STANDING TALL
The Kevin Everett Story

Sam Carchidi

TRIUMPH
BOOKS

CONTENTS

DEDICATION

To the best team a writer could have by his side, my family—
my wife, JoAnn; my daughter, Sara; my son, Sammy; and
my mother-in-law, Maryann. I would also like to dedicate
this book to the thousands of spinal-cord patients (and
their families) who courageously battle their condition in
anonymity. Your determination is my inspiration.

ACKNOWLEDGMENTS

There are so many people to thank for making this inspiring project a reality; so many people who unselfishly gave their time so this story could be told with the detail and care that it deserves.

My only fear is that I will inadvertently omit someone. If I do, please forgive my ignorance.

First, I would like to thank Kevin Everett and his fiancée, Wiande Moore, for allowing me into their lives. My life is much more enriched because of our time together. Thanks for your openness, your grace, and your humor, guys, and a special thanks to Wiande for sharing her invaluable journal.

Thanks are also in order for members of Kevin's and Wiande's families. Patricia Dugas (Kevin's mom) is an amazing woman, and I can see where Kevin gets his inner strength and courage. Also, a special thanks to Kevin's sisters: Davia, who is also a profile in courage; Herchell; and Kelli.

Mamawa Moore, Wiande's mom, was also kind with her time, as was Wayetu Moore, Wiande's sister.

I'd also like to thank James "Junior" Nico, Kevin's personable grandfather, along with his aunt, Jackie Adams, and his cousin, Chris Adams.

Many thanks to Al Celaya, Jimmy Rieves, and Mario Cristobal, three of Kevin's former football coaches, and to Tony Tompkins, one of Kevin's high school teammates.

This project could not have been completed without the generous cooperation from the staff at Memorial Hermann|TIRR (The Institute of Rehabilitation and Research) in Houston, including Dr. Teodoro "Ted" Castillo, Dr. William Donovan, Rafferty Laredo, Darryn Atkinson, Dawn Brown, Worth Whiteside, Barbara Jackson, Liza Criswell, and Alejandra Rodriguez.

I could not be more appreciative of Dr. Kevin Gibbons, supervisor of neurosurgery at Millard Fillmore Gates Hospital in Buffalo, for going beyond the call of duty to help sort through numerous medical details. Thanks also to Mike Hughes of the hospital's public-relations department.

Members of the Buffalo Bills organization were also a major help—and their love and admiration for Kevin became oh, so clear. I would like to thank Andrew Cappuccino, the Bills' orthopedist; head coach Dick Jauron; and club executives Tom Modrak, Paul Lancaster, Marv Levy (who stepped down as GM after the season), and Scott Berchtold. Several Bills players also deserve mention, including Robert Royal, Roscoe Parrish, Brian Moorman, John McCargo, Trent Edwards, Mario Haggan, Jabari Greer, J.P. Losman, Lee Evans, Matt Murphy, Marshawn Lynch, and Bryan Scott. Domenik Hixon, who started the season with the Denver Broncos and ended it with the New York Giants, also deserves thanks.

I want to thank Adam Taliaferro and Dean Ragone—two courageous men who didn't let spinal injuries slow them down—for sharing their heartwarming stories.

I would be remiss if I didn't thank Eric Armstead and Brandon Strauss from E.O. Sports Management; Derek Boyko and Ryan Nissan of the Philadelphia Eagles' public-relations department; Scott Brown of the *Pittsburgh Tribune-Review*; and two patients from TIRR in Houston, Virgil Calhoun and Amanda Brugmann. Thanks also to Virgil's wife, Lyn, for her help, and to NFL players James Harrison of the Pittsburgh Steelers and Takeo Spikes of the Philadelphia Eagles.

Several people from the Miami Project were also helpful, including Dr. Barth Green, Marc Buoniconti, Nick Buoniconti, and Scott Roy.

This project was jump-started because of the work provided by Kathy McHugh, whose transcribing was much-appreciated.

I'd also like to thank my employer, *The Philadelphia Inquirer*, for granting me the time to work on this project—specifically, editors John Quinn, Gary Miles, and Jason Carris.

And I can't forget my wonderful family for their love and encouragement. Their support motivated me during the 18-hour workdays.

Finally, I would like to thank the great folks at Triumph Books—especially Tom Bast, Don Gulbrandsen, and Mitch Rogatz—for believing in this book and making it come to fruition. Your vision should be commended.

INTRODUCTION

As Kevin Everett lay in a Buffalo hospital bed, hooked to tubes and machines that were helping him breathe, the world was told the grim news: he may not live, and he almost certainly will never walk again.

The minute the doctor gave us that startling update, Kevin Everett, a third-year tight end with the Buffalo Bills, became America's Player.

America loves underdogs.

America loves following the progress of injured, ill, or handicapped athletes who are fighting nearly insurmountable odds.

Brian Piccolo, Tony Conigliaro, and Dave Dravecky.

Lance Armstrong, Dennis Byrd, and Adam Taliaferro.

Jim Abbott, Alonzo Mourning, and Jon Lester.

Those are just some of the athletes who struck a chord with Americans because of their indomitable spirit, their courage, their resiliency.

Kevin Everett, 25, wasn't trying to put his name on the list, wasn't trying to become a hero, wasn't trying to become an everlasting symbol of hope for spinal patients.

But when he tackled a Denver Broncos kickoff returner and became paralyzed on September 9, 2007, his story was just starting. So was his new life.

When his longtime girlfriend, Wiande, first saw him in the hospital, she dropped her belongings and grabbed the railing on Kevin's bed to keep from collapsing. As a little girl, Wiande had survived a civil war in Liberia and had experienced a bullet whizzing between her and her cousin, but that couldn't compare to the fear she now felt.

The fear was shared by Kevin's mom, Patricia, who a month earlier had undergone a similar hospital vigil when her 11-year-old daughter fell into a diabetic coma.

Kevin, Wiande, and Patricia. They would be at the crux of the recovery attempt, but there would be many others, including an affable 56-year-old hospital patient named Virgil Calhoun, who would become an unlikely part of the story.

It is a story that transcends sports, a story about how Kevin's girlfriend—a West African–born former track All-American, who met Kevin at the University of Miami—and his devoted mother never left the side of the man they love.

It is a story about how the Buffalo Bills would never let their fallen teammate out of their minds. Never.

It is a story about how a relatively new and controversial cooling treatment—hypothermia—was used in Kevin's recovery attempt.

And, quite simply, it is a story that brought a little-known tight end into the hearts of America. Forever.

CHAPTER 1

"SHOW ME A SIGN"

"When someone gets hit on the field, that's the No. 1 thing

they want to do—put the thumb up

to let everyone know it's not that bad.

But I couldn't do it."

They joined hands and formed a circle. Some bowed their heads. Some looked to the heavens and pleaded softly.

"Please, God, help him get up," Robert Royal said to himself.

It was a strange place to be praying. This wasn't a cathedral with stained-glass windows, holy statues, and a marble altar.

This was Ralph Wilson Stadium in Orchard Park, New York, just outside Buffalo. On the field, National Football League players from the Buffalo Bills and Denver Broncos locked fingers in a prayer circle and watched anxiously as medical personnel attended to Kevin Everett. The popular third-year Bills tight end who twitched for a few seconds as he attempted to get up now seemed comatose as he lay on the turf.

Royal, who was also one of the Buffalo Bills' tight ends, was in the middle of the prayer circle. Like the rest of the players, the sight of his powerfully built friend—"K.E." to most of his teammates—lying on the ground startled him.

For most of his teenage and adult life, Everett could do just about any athletic feat he wanted: dunk a basketball, leap over a 6'8" high-jump bar, bench-press 375 pounds in the weight room. But now, at age 25, his chiseled 6-foot-4, 255-pound body wouldn't listen to his mind's simple request: Pick yourself up and walk to the sideline.

Everett had fallen to the ground face-first after tackling Denver kick returner Domenik Hixon to start the second half. He lay motionless for nearly 15 minutes, thoughts of paralysis dancing through his head.

"I'm done," Everett sensed when he couldn't respond to the Buffalo trainer's request to move his limbs. "I'm going to be paralyzed."

About 1,500 miles south in suburban Houston, Kevin's mom, Patricia Dugas, watched the scene in horror on a big-screen TV at a sports bar.

Wiande Moore, his longtime girlfriend, was temporarily spared the agony. A former scholarship track athlete, she had met Kevin when they attended the University of Miami. Oblivious to the develop-

"I'm done. I'm going to be paralyzed."

ments in Buffalo, she was having her 2006 silver Honda Accord washed in Texas at the time of the injury.

Soon, the agony would engulf the trio. Soon, the agony would spread beyond Texas and western New York. Soon, a doctor was using words such as "catastrophic," "permanent neurological paralysis," and "potentially lethal" when discussing the spinal-cord injury.

❖❖❖

Before her family moved to America when she was seven years old, Wiande (pronounced WEE-Ahn-DEE) Moore grew up in West Africa in the middle of a civil war. She remembers seeing dead bodies in the street near her home in Liberia. She remembers the frequent sound of gunshots and the time a bullet whizzed between her and her cousin. But nothing could compare to the fear she would soon feel when discovering that Kevin—her best friend, the love of her life—was motionless and that she was helpless, far away from the man she adored.

Wiande, 24, had gone to church that morning in Texas. She planned to watch the game with Kevin's mom, Patricia—whom Wiande calls "Mrs. Patricia"—and Kevin's three young sisters, Herchell, 15, Kelli, 14, and Davia, 11. Kevin had bought a home, located in the Houston suburb of Humble, for the family the previous year, and he also lived there.

That day, Wiande was running late. She had her car washed and was getting ready to make the 10-minute drive to Humble when Kevin's mom called and told her the Bills' game wasn't on local TV. They would have to watch it at a local bar and restaurant, also located in Humble. A short time later, Wiande received a call from her cousin, and the news wasn't good—Kevin had just been injured and was still on the field.

Frantically, Wiande headed to Kevin's house.

"My heart immediately begins to panic and in my mind, I don't know what to do," Wiande wrote in her journal later that night. She is a tenth-grade English teacher and track coach at her high school alma mater in Texas, and writing is her passion. She has written journals throughout her life; it is her way to stay organized, her way to preserve the past. "The drive to Kevin's was more of a panic than anything. Around 1:30, Mrs. Patricia called my phone from Mulligan's sports bar and said ... 'I don't know how critical it is, but he's down on the ground and can't get up.'"

"I have to talk to somebody about what's going on with my baby."

Wiande figured that instead of meeting with Mrs. Patricia at the sports bar, she would comfort Kevin's three young sisters at their house.

"As tears continued to roll down my face and the rain from the windows dramatically fell on my windshield, I knew this accident was life-threatening," Wiande wrote in a journal that had the NFL logo on the navy blue cover. "I arrived at Kevin's house so afraid and scared. My mind was trying to stay strong for his sisters and mama, but I couldn't stand the thought of this happening to him and he's so far away. What is he thinking? How is he feeling? I couldn't think about anything, but I had to get to him. I had to get to him."

As she drove to Kevin's house, Wiande received another call from Kevin's mom, who was still at the sports bar. Things didn't look good, she said. Wiande pulled to the side of the road, wiped her eyes, and composed herself before continuing to Kevin's house to be with his three sisters.

When she arrived at the house, Davia, Kevin's youngest sister, was wiping tears as she opened the door for Wiande.

"It's going to be okay," said Wiande, a twinge of her West African accent noticeable. "It's going to be all right."

About five minutes later, Patricia arrived at the house and searched madly for emergency phone numbers for anyone who could shed light on the situation.

"I have to talk to somebody about what's going on with my baby," Patricia said to no one in particular. "I need to find out what's going on with my baby."

It was the second recent jolt to Patricia's warm, engaging family. The previous month, Davia went into a diabetic coma and spent two weeks in the intensive-care unit of a Texas hospital.

Now her oldest son appeared to be in an even worse predicament.

❧ ❧ ❧

About one and a half hours before the injury, Everett had made one of the few starts of his three-year career, lining up at tight end in the season opener for both teams. This looked to be a breakthrough season for Everett. He had missed his entire rookie season because of a torn ligament in his left knee, and he was still playing catch-up in his second year. But now, in his third season, he felt more comfortable with the offensive system. He felt as if he belonged, felt as if he would make his mark—just like he did in high school, in junior college, and at the University of Miami.

The Bills had approached the season with guarded optimism. The team hoped to improve on a 7–9 season, basing a lot of its expectations on the emergence of quarterback J.P. Losman and the talents of wide receiver Lee Evans, along with a rebuilt offensive line and the additions of running back Marshawn Lynch and linebacker Paul Posluszny, two talented rookies.

In the offseason, the players were hanging out more than usual. They were getting to know each other, getting more comfortable together. That closeness, they believed, would carry onto the field and produce a good season. The media was saying the Bills had a young team and that not much was expected of them. The players were intent on proving them wrong.

The optimism that came with the new season soon turned into fear. Fear that Everett would never be able to move again. Fear that he would spend the rest of his life in a wheelchair. Fear that his future might not last very long.

Everett had been on hundreds of kickoff-coverage teams at the high school, collegiate, and professional level. On this fateful day, as the Bills' Rian Lindell teed up the second-half kickoff, Everett was the first player to the kicker's right.

As he raced downfield, Everett wasn't blocked by anyone and had a clear shot at tackling Hixon, who was cutting toward the outside. Everett closed ground and, with his upper body leaning forward, collided with Hixon. Everett's helmet violently met the side of Hixon's helmet and shoulder pads near the Denver 20-yard line.

Besides the life-changing hit, there was something oddly different about the kickoff.

"They didn't want to block me," Everett recalled, more than three months after the play. "I guess they watched on film how I run into guys."

In football parlance, Everett was usually the wedge-buster, a guy who races downfield and throws his body into a cluster of blockers in an attempt to clog the lanes for the kick returner. It's dangerous work, but somebody has to do it.

On this play, though, Everett's job was made surprisingly easy.

Royal, a fellow tight end, bobbed up and down on the Bills' sideline as he watched the play unfold, gleeful that his good friend, Everett, was zipping past potential blockers.

"I was excited because he was representing the tight ends and he was the first one downfield," Royal said.

"I had the feeling their big wedge guys didn't want to have any contact with me, because I ran right straight to the guy," Everett said, referring to the kick returner, Hixon. "And the outside blocker, he didn't even come toward me, which I found odd. So I had a clear path to the guy. I was like, 'Wow, I've never had this much (room),' and I got excited about it, too. I guess I put too much thought into it...and the worst happened."

"They didn't want to block me. I guess they watched on film how I run into guys."

Hixon was driven sideways by Everett's impact and was falling to the artificial turf when another Buffalo player finished the tackle.

"My body," Everett said, "went numb. It felt like he ran straight through me. I wanted to reach out and grab him, but I couldn't move."

As Bills quarterback Losman watched Everett placed on a backboard that would be moved into an ambulance, he hoped his teammate would give a reassuring gesture.

"Show me a sign," Losman thought to himself, a feeling shared by 71,132 fans and the TV audience.

Everett wanted to give a "thumbs-up" gesture to those at the stadium—like the Detroit Lions' Mike Utley famously did when he was carted off the field, paralyzed, in a 1991 game. Kevin wanted to show his mom, his girlfriend, his three young sisters, and the man who helped raise him, his grandfather, that everything was all right.

"When someone gets hit on the field, that's the No. 1 thing they want to do—put the thumb up to let everyone know it's not that bad," he said. "But I couldn't do it."

He couldn't move anything.

"I was trying," Everett said.

Everett was conscious while the medical crew attended to him.

"I knew what had happened the whole time I was out there," Everett said. "I heard the fans screaming and then I heard them get quiet. I knew everything that was going on. I heard my teammates telling me to get up and I couldn't. I'm glad they didn't try to help me up."

Moving him could have caused more damage to the spinal cord.

Everett heard a potpourri of voices; some belonged to his teammates, others to the Bills' quick-acting medical team, which, nine days earlier, had practiced for situations just like this.

Many of the players from the Bills and Broncos joined hands and said a prayer. "I didn't think it was serious. I thought it was a normal football injury," said Roscoe Parrish, a Bills wide receiver and one of Everett's closest friends. But the longer Everett didn't move, the more Parrish's concern grew.

They took turns touching different parts of Kevin's body, asking if he could feel anything. He couldn't.

"I just started praying and hoping," said Parrish, who had also been Kevin's teammate at the University of Miami, "that everything would be OK."

Everett felt some minor discomfort in his neck, but everything else was numb.

"Actually, I felt like it was all over," Everett said. "On the impact, I felt that everything just shut down. I couldn't move anything. I tried, with every strength I had in my body, to get up,

and I couldn't get up. And I just felt like, 'Wow, I am actually paralyzed, because I had never had a stinger that made me feel like I
couldn't move anything, so I knew it was a big problem when I
couldn't lift my arms or move my legs. I tried, with everything I
had in my mind, to move my body, but I couldn't do it."

Buffalo's medical team sprang into action. Swiftly.

Bud Carpenter, the Bills' head trainer, raced to Kevin's side.

"Can you move anything?" Carpenter asked.

"No. Nothing," Everett said.

"Oh, man," Everett remembered Carpenter saying.

Carpenter signaled for some assistance. Dr. John Marzo, the
team's medical director, and assistant trainer Chris Fischetti hurried
onto the field.

They took turns touching different parts of Kevin's body,
asking if he could feel anything.

He couldn't.

The medical team determined that Kevin, whose eyes remained open, had no mobility below his neck. Fischetti waved for
Dr. Andrew Cappuccino, the Bills' orthopedist.

Cappuccino performed some more tests, squeezing various
parts of Kevin's body and asking him to respond. Nothing.
Cappuccino swallowed hard. This wasn't a typical football injury.
This was life-threatening. Cappuccino determined that Kevin was
quadriplegic, which meant he had zero voluntary muscle function
in his arms and legs. He turned to Carpenter, the trainer, and told
him they were in their "spinal-cord drill."

Carpenter immobilized Kevin's neck. Thirteen minutes after
his collision with Hixon, Everett was gingerly placed into the
ambulance, which literally shook because of the crowd's loud,
thunderous cheers. A few minutes later, while on a backboard in
the ambulance, Everett was intravenously given a steroid called
Solu-Medrol to protect the spinal cord and reduce its swelling.

At the same time, Cappuccino sent iced saline into Kevin's veins, flushing the body to lower his temperature—a ground-breaking treatment known as moderate hypothermia.

"I'm having trouble breathing," Kevin said as the ambulance headed to Millard Fillmore Gates Hospital, located about 25 minutes away.

"Hang in there," Cappuccino told him, masking his own fright.

Everett said he doesn't remember much pain. Nor does he remember receiving treatment in the ambulance. In fact, aside from what took place on the field in the minutes after the collision, he remembers very little about the first two days after his injury.

As the ambulance drove toward the hospital, no one knew if Kevin would ever return to the field.

No one knew if he would live.

❖❖❖

Buffalo lost the opener, 15–14, when Denver's Jason Elam kicked a 42-yard field goal as time expired.

It was the Bills' second jolt of the day. The first one—the sight of Everett being knocked motionless and then driven away in an ambulance—would have the most lasting effect.

The Buffalo locker room was somber when the media entered after the game.

"When we came in here, the first thing we thought about was Kevin," Buffalo wide receiver Evans said. "There are things that are bigger than the game and that's certainly an example."

"I hope it's the last time I ever have to choke back tears in the middle of the playing field," Bills punter Brian Moorman said. "We're in a waiting period and hoping we get good news."

"Football isn't what's important now," said Royal, the tight end who is one of Kevin's best friends.

Everett likely experienced about two-thirds of a ton of compression force on his spine when he made the hit, Dr. Timothy

Gay told *USA Today*. Dr. Gay, a professor of physics at the University of Nebraska-Lincoln who has studied the physics of football, said kickoffs produce more violent collisions than almost any play in football because players have more of a chance to get to their full speed.

Gay watched slow-motion replays of the hit and said it appeared Everett's head was down when he made the tackle. That means the force of the collision was applied to his spine.

"I think I had my head down more so than other times when I would make a tackle," Everett agreed.

Football players are taught a basic tackling premise: To avoid injuries, keep your head up. It's not always easy to do. There are unseen variables that cause players to slip or twist at odd angles when they make a tackle, thus increasing the risk of injury.

With the head down, the spine is more vulnerable.

"That's why you don't go flying at a guy without your head up," said Gay, adding he didn't think more protective equipment would have helped Everett because of his head's angle at the point of impact. "You have 250-pound guys running 10 feet per second into each other. You're putting yourself in a dangerous position. "

❖❖❖

Everett's injury jolted Jimmy Rieves, his former junior college coach at Kilgore, Texas. It caused Rieves to take an unwanted trip in his memory—back to 1989 when he was a graduate assistant at the University of Mississippi and Ole Miss defensive back Chucky Mullins was severely injured in a game against Vanderbilt.

Eighteen years later, watching Everett collapse face-first to the turf seemed like a grim instant replay to Rieves.

"It brought back the same images," Rieves said, "because of the way they fell to the ground when the contact was made. It was like deja vu."

Mullins, a Mississippi defensive back, broke up a pass and collided violently with Vanderbilt running back Brad Gaines. The collision shattered four vertebrae in Mullins' neck, leaving him paralyzed from the neck down.

Plagued by recurring respiratory complications from the injury, Mullins died less than three years later.

Rieves, who stopped coaching in 2006 and is now Kilgore's director of student development and the junior college's assistant athletic director, was observing from the press box with Mississippi's defensive coordinator when Mullins was injured. "My job was to watch the other team's offense, so I saw the whole play develop," he said. "Chucky was defending a pass and went up to make a tip when contact was made."

"Don't worry about me, mama. I'm all right. I love you all."

Rieves said it will take a while before he gets the image of a collapsing Everett out of his mind.

"I knew it was serious from the way Kevin fell," he said. "He just went limp when he was falling down, without even trying to catch himself. It looked like a tree falling."

He has many other memories of Everett, whom he coached for two years at Kilgore Junior College.

Rieves called Everett a "coach's dream" and described him as a hard worker who never got in trouble off the field. Now, the soft-spoken, polite young man—who was raised by his mom in a mostly single-parent home and served as a role model for his three young sisters—was paralyzed from the shoulders down and fighting for his life after being transported to Millard Fillmore Gates Hospital in downtown Buffalo.

Later that night, Everett went through four hours of surgery after it was determined that he had suffered a dislocation of the third and fourth cervical vertebrae. Cappuccino, who specializes in spine injuries, tried to explain the injury in layman's terms. The vertebrae of the spine "line up like box cars of a train," he said, adding that the third cervical vertebra had shifted completely over the front of the fourth cervical vertebra, causing a scissoring effect of the spinal cord.

In other words, a train wreck of the spine.

Before the surgery, before his third and fourth vertebrae were fused together, Kevin talked to his mom on a cell phone.

"Don't worry about me, mama. I'm all right. I love you all," he said.

"I'm getting there as fast as I can," said Patricia, trying to hide the trepidation in her voice. "I love you, baby."

Patricia Dugas, 45, a single mom for most of her adult life, hung up the phone and couldn't stop crying. She never went to sleep that night, staying awake to pack, pray, and be at the airport long before the sun rose the next morning.

Everett's spinal surgery, performed by Cappuccino and Dr. Kevin Gibbons, was done in two parts. The first involved the placement of a bone graft, a small cage, a plate, and four screws used to repair the dislocation. The second part, which left a six-inch scar at the base of his neck, included the placement of four screws and two small rods used to fixate the spine. "The spine was decompressed, or the pressure was relieved," Cappuccino said.

After he performed the surgery, Cappuccino described Everett's chances of full recovery as "bleak" and painted a grim picture.

"I believe there will be some permanent neurological paralysis," he said.

Cappuccino said the spinal cord was not severed, but he tempered that optimistic news by saying Everett faced several life-threatening conditions, including respiratory failure, blood clotting, and infection.

He called it a "potentially catastrophic" injury.

Football collisions rarely cause deaths. According to the National Safety Council, a person is far more likely to die from being struck by lightning than from being struck against another individual.

But Kevin was battling to stay alive now, and you could feel the pain in the words Wiande penned in her journal.

"After a while, we spoke with the doctors from Buffalo," she wrote, putting Dr. Cappuccino's name in parentheses, "and he spoke with Mrs. Patricia about undergoing surgery on Kevin's third/fourth vertebrae. Before the surgery, Kevin spoke with us and told his mama he loves her and his sisters and me. The look of worry on Mrs. Patricia's face was my only focus. The tears rolling down his sisters' faces, especially Davia's, were my only concern. We booked a flight for 6 AM the next morning on Delta Airlines. This wasn't the first time I was anxious to see my love, but this was the first time I knew I had to be the stronger half for the both of us. I laid in the bed that we always share our thoughts...always spend our time together with laughter, tears and joy. All these memories in my head made my mind wander. I looked at our picture on the dresser and kissed my baby on the forehead, wishing he was there with me like always. I read my Bible, said my prayers, and thanked God for saving his life, and then closed my eyes."

CHAPTER 2
ROLE MODEL

"I've been in this business a long time and I've seen
the things kids do, the way they walk
and they way they talk, and I'll tell you,
this kid had class. I always thought he was a
little different than everybody else. He came
from a tough neighborhood, but he
always had a class about him."

Being the man of the house isn't easy for someone not yet a teenager, but Kevin Everett seemed natural at it. He changed his baby sisters' diapers, bathed them, boiled their bottles, mixed their formula, and playfully crawled after them.

He may have been a man among boys when he played football at Thomas Jefferson High in Port Arthur, Texas, but at home, he was a teddy bear of a big brother.

"He just took on so much responsibility because he loved them so much," said Patricia Dugas, Kevin's mom.

Kevin's birth dad never lived with the family, and his mom married Herchel Dugas when Kevin was seven years old. Patricia and Herchel had three girls. Kevin became protective of them and took on a father-figure role, as his stepfather frequently was out of the picture.

There were a lot of breakups, Patricia Dugas said of her relationship with her husband.

Not having a dad to lean on, Kevin reached out to James "Junior" Nico, his grandfather and Patricia Dugas's father.

Junior became the father Kevin never had, became the man who set him on a straight-and-narrow path, the man who taught him to be responsible for his actions and to never be bitter about life.

"He was my father figure. My dad was really never around, never really around at all," Kevin said. "I sort of looked to my grandfather. He basically did everything for me in my life, as far as taking care of me and showing me the love he would show to a son. I got closer and closer to him."

"When Kevin came into this world," Patricia said, "he shared my daddy with me. My daddy was *his* daddy. My daddy loves his Kevin, and he took good care of Kevin. He helped a whole lot with my son and took on that position as a father to my son."

Junior was always there for Kevin. Always. In fact, Junior

assisted Kevin when he took his first steps as an infant.

"My dad stood him up and he took two steps and fell on his butt," said Patricia, her laughter growing with each word. "I ran over there and picked him up and started hugging and kissing him because I was so proud."

Years later, when Kevin was having what he called "family issues" at home, he moved in with Junior and his grandmother, Anita Nico, during his elementary and high school days. "I was back and forth," Kevin said.

He moved in permanently with his grandparents when he was 14. "I wasn't seeing eye to eye on some things and felt it was the best thing to do," Kevin said. "And my grandfather thought so, too. Everybody in the family came to an agreement on it."

"He basically did everything for me in my life, as far as taking care of me and showing me the love he would show to a son."

Even though he lived away from home, he stayed close with his mom and his sisters, never breaking their bond. His grandmother was the disciplinarian in the family. "She didn't play games. She stood behind her word and her word was what it was. There was no negotiation about it," said Kevin, smiling softly. "If you didn't follow her rules, she punished you. And we loved her for it because most of us turned out pretty decent."

Her cooking was more than decent. Kevin calls it the best he has ever eaten. His brown eyes arch skyward, like he's discussing something heavenly, when he talks about her concoction of red beans, sausage, and bacon, or something she called "Smothered Chicken." Smothered in brown gravy and onions, seconds were natural. And sometimes thirds.

After Kevin's grandmother lost a battle with cancer and died during Kevin's junior year in high school, the teenager's connection with his grandfather grew even stronger.

Junior rarely attended Kevin's high school athletic events—he always seemed to be working or battling an ailment, such as diabetes or high blood pressure—but that didn't matter to his grandson. His grandfather was always Kevin's confidant, always someone he could count on, always someone to steer him in the right direction.

"He's funny, very loving, outspoken, and fun to be around," Kevin said. "He loves to talk. A people's person. Everybody who meets him or knows him, they love him to death."

Sort of what people say when they meet Kevin Everett.

❖ ❖ ❖

Junior Nico was the father Kevin never had. He was there to help Kevin take his first steps and there to help him ride his first bike. He would take Kevin fishing and, occasionally, to the rodeo, or they would sit together on the front porch of his three-bedroom Port Arthur house and talk about life. Junior would explain what makes a good man.

His heart ached terribly as he prayed for his fishing buddy's recovery.

"I'd say, 'Son, always be the best you can,'" he recalled. "'No matter what you do in life, do the best you can with what you got.'"

Junior, a broad-shouldered man with a 6'1" frame, did the best he could. He was a heavy-machine operator for as long as he can remember. Junior would load ships from the docks, hang steel at an oil refinery, pull up items (and, sometimes, dead bodies) from overturned boats. "Anything that had to do with a machine, I did it."

Junior and his wife raised eight children. Kevin and some of their other grandsons also lived at their home for long periods of time. "We'd throw mattresses down in the dining room so everyone had a place to sleep," Junior said.

As a preschooler, Kevin followed his grandfather everywhere. Junior would work in the garden, and Kevin, wearing his trademark white fishing hat, would be right behind, always interested in his grandfather's endeavors, always smiling. Junior bought Kevin a tiny rake and shovel, and the two became a gardening duo, one in his mid-fifties, the other just five years old.

"Me and him became close since before he could walk or crawl," Junior said.

With his wife cooking lovingly inside the house, Junior would hold Kevin and rock him on the front porch. If Junior had a dime for each time Kevin fell asleep in his arms, well, he'd probably be a rich man.

Kevin always seemed to have a smile for his grandfather.

"They know love when they see it," Junior said. "Even at that young age."

Years later, when Kevin wasn't with his grandfather, he was playing with the neighborhood kids or helping his grandmother.

"He's always had a wonderful personality," Junior said. "Never been in any trouble. I've never known him to drink. He's always been an important part of my life."

And so as Junior, 76, watched the replay of the tackle that left Kevin paralyzed, his heart ached terribly as he prayed for his fishing buddy's recovery.

"Oh, man, it was devastating when I found out the seriousness of it," he said.

❖ ❖ ❖

Kevin grew up in gritty Port Arthur—located in southeast Texas, 90 miles east of Houston and 250 miles west of New Orleans—where oil refining was king. If you lived in Port Arthur, chances were that someone in your family—or someone you knew—worked at one of its oil refineries.

Wherever you worked, you were likely to attend one of the high school football games on Friday night. High school football was a deeply rooted part of the Texas culture, and Kevin Everett couldn't wait until the day he could play for the Yellow Jackets of Port Arthur Thomas Jefferson High.

In his youth, Kevin was bigger than most of the neighborhood kids and always weighed too much to play in the youth leagues. He didn't get his first taste of organized football until he was an eighth grader at Thomas Edison Junior High.

Aside from Everett, Edison's team didn't exactly look imposing. In fact, Everett playfully belittled the team's makeup during signups.

"He looked around the gym and said to me, 'Look at all these small guys. We won't win a game,'" recalled Tony Tompkins.

Tompkins was not amused. He was the quarterback—and one of the team's little guys, perhaps a foot smaller than Kevin, who was then 6'3".

Tompkins remembered feeling angered by Everett's dismissal of the team's "small guys."

"I didn't say anything when he made the comment," Tompkins said, "but I didn't like him. I thought he didn't respect some guys."

He paused.

"But after a few games, he was my main target," Tompkins added, smiling, "and he changed my mind."

Everett also changed his projection about his team. Edison went undefeated and won a district title.

"We just had a connection together," Everett said about his quarterback and inseparable friend. "In eighth grade, we had all the high school coaches in the area coming to watch me and him. It was amazing to see all of them lined up on the sideline. They do a lot of recruiting and try to get the best athletes early. They go to the middle school and try to pinpoint the guys they want to come to their high school. But, with me, I knew I was going to Port Arthur."

He wanted to follow in the footsteps of his football-playing cousins who had attended the school, "and I liked the tradition they had over there."

Kevin Everett couldn't wait until the day he could play for the Yellow Jackets.

Everett and Tompkins both attended Port Arthur Thomas Jefferson High School. They became close friends and, years later, would both play professional football—Tompkins, an accomplished kick returner who is known as "Magic," has played in Canada the last three years—and would live together in the offseason.

"He's my main boy," Everett said. "He's one of my road dogs."

When Tompkins' mother was dying in 2007, Everett made it a point to do something with his friend when he wasn't at the hospital.

"I had to get his mind off things," Kevin said.

They would shoot pool and talk. Seeing his mom fade away was taking its toll on Tompkins. Kevin tried to ease his friend's pain.

"I'd be going to the hospital every day, and every weekend if I got a chance, we'd get together and talk. It definitely helped," Tompkins said. "He went through the same thing when his grandmother passed, so he had experience in losing a close relative. He knew what it felt like, and it was his loss, too, because he was close with my mom when she was alive."

Tompkins' mom, Tangela, was in hospitals in Houston and Port Arthur for about a year and a half before losing her battle with colon cancer.

❖❖❖

A two-way end, Everett was a three-year starter on both sides of the ball at tradition-rich Thomas Jefferson High. He had a dominating season as a junior and an even better one as a senior. Everett forced six fumbles as a senior, a season that also included 14 tackles for losses and more than 300 receiving yards—enough to make him an all-state Class 5A selection.

Kevin's senior season was an emotional one. During the preseason, head coach Richard Marler had suffered a heart attack and was in a coma. Al Celaya, one of Marler's assistants, assumed the head-coaching duties.

"He was in a coma the whole season," Celaya recalled. "We went to the state playoffs that year and he remained in a coma the entire time. We lost our playoff game and our season ended on a Saturday—and he died a few days later. It was almost like he stayed around the entire season for us, and after we lost, he kind of let go."

Thomas Jefferson High, which is now known as Memorial, finished with an admirable 7–4 record that season. Kevin led the way.

"He had all kinds of recruiting attention that year," Celaya said. "Kevin was the type of player who wanted the football in his hands because of the unbelievable things he could do with it. He was 6'4" and 225 or 230 pounds and the guy moved around like a wideout. That's the kind of player he was. In the offseason, Kevin was the baddest player we had on the team."

Translation: No one worked harder in the weight room than Everett, and no one could match his intensity in drills.

"No one could whip Kevin Everett," Celaya said. "Many tried, but no one could take him in offseason competition drills. Any one-on-one drill we did, he won. Kevin Everett was in a class by himself. And it didn't matter what side of the ball he played. He dominated on both sides."

When Kevin was a senior, Jefferson High began winning games after Celaya moved Tompkins from tailback to quarterback midway through the year. "Tony was one of our better athletes; he ran a 4.5 (40-yard dash), and we wanted to get the ball in his hands," Celaya said.

Kevin was his favorite target, but Jefferson relied primarily on its ground game. Kevin's blocking was a key.

"Tony was a Vince Young-type, a quarterback who was a threat to run," Celaya said.

Tony, Kevin, and sophomore running back James Johnson triggered the offense.

The defense had Kevin as its anchor, and college coaches were divided as to which side of the ball he was best suited to play.

"Kevin was quiet, but he became the team leader because he was the best player," said Celaya,

No one worked harder in the weight room than Everett, and no one could match his intensity in drills.

who is now an assistant coach at a high school in Beaumont, Texas. "Everybody who faced him knew that if you could stop Kevin Everett, you could make a name for yourself and could be a somebody."

Celaya said there was "something about the way Kevin carried himself" that indicated he was headed for stardom.

"I've been in this business a long time and I've seen the things kids do, the way they walk and the way they talk, and I'll tell you, this kid had class," Celaya said. "I always thought he was a little different than everybody else. He came from a tough neighborhood, but he always had a class about him."

Everett remembers Celaya talking to him after practice in his senior season.

"One day," Celaya told him, "you're going to be playing on Sundays."

"I kind of just brushed it off," Everett said.

But he never forgot the words.

Kevin also never forgot how Celaya cared for the players and molded them into a cohesive unit. "He was just a great guy," Everett said. "He always wanted the best for all of us, always pushed us to do our best and enforced hard work—you know, he got on your tail when you were doing bad and he was there to tell you when you were doing good, too, so he wasn't a strict disciplinarian."

While attending Thomas Jefferson, Everett excelled in sports other than football. He began his high-school track career as a sprinter, but he didn't like all the running that was done in practice, so he switched and became a high jumper as a senior. He quickly became a standout in the event, even if he didn't look so graceful. He cleared 6'8" with a style that took advantage of his vertical leap—and not his form.

"I was actually sitting over the bar going over it, instead of using the technique of a high jumper," he said.

Everett also dominated in basketball. A three-year starter at power forward, he averaged about 16 points, 10 rebounds, and five blocks per game during his senior year, becoming one of the region's most talked-about dunk artists.

Kevin enjoyed the sport, but nothing compared to his love for football.

❖ ❖ ❖

Growing up in Port Arthur, Texas, Chris Adams wasn't only Kevin's first cousin; he was also his best friend.

"He's just like my little brother," Kevin said. "Growing up, we were together every single day."

Chris was nearly three years younger than Kevin and looked

up to his cousin. They'd play football, ride bikes, and hang out
with their grandmother, Anita Nico. When Anita died, Chris
moved in with his grandfather and shared a bedroom with Kevin.

"I was working out of town a lot, and it worked out better,"
said Jackie Adams, Chris's mom. "Chris and Kevin always did
things together. Chris got along better with Kevin than he did his
own brother. Brothers are always fighting, but I never saw Chris
and Kevin ever have an argument. Everything was always hunky-
dory with them. Everything was cool."

They were football teammates for one year in high school,
while Kevin was being recruited by a flock of scouts. Virtually
every college in the country showed interest, some stronger than
others. In the end, Everett narrowed his choices to Miami, Florida,
and Auburn.

Everett had always been enamored with Miami, primarily
because he loved watching wide receiver Michael Irvin play there.
On his recruiting visit to Miami, Everett proudly posed for a photo
next to the Heisman Trophy that had been won by Hurricanes
quarterback Vinny Testaverde in 1986.

But Everett couldn't qualify to play at Miami because of a poor
grade in English. He would have to bide time at a junior college
for two seasons, get his grades in order, and then transfer to
Miami. That was the plan.

It worked perfectly. In each of his seasons at Kilgore College,
located about 250 miles north of Kevin's hometown, Everett
earned first-team All-Southwest Junior College Conference honors.
One scouting service rated him as the second-best junior-college
player in the nation. He also was hitting the books.

Jimmy Rieves said Everett was a role model for Kilgore's
players.

"Junior college is for young men who have messed up
academically or need to be looked over," said Rieves, who was

Kilgore's head coach from 2000 to 2006. "They're not outlaws. We have good kids, but sometimes, they're immature. But Kevin was mature when he got there. He didn't have to grow up. He was a man when he got there and it was nice to have someone there like that."

Grandpa Nico had taught Kevin well.

Everett buckled down in the classroom and was the football team's unquestioned leader in the weight room, Rieves said. "You never had to worry that Kevin would slack off and wouldn't work," he said. "He wasn't a rah-rah guy. He was a quiet leader and he pushed himself in the weight room. When we had players who weren't mentally strong, we'd put them in the weight room with Kevin because we knew he'd push them and they wouldn't slack off."

It took Everett just one and a half years to graduate from the junior college. "You have to be working hard in the classroom to do that because our academic standards are tough," Rieves said.

Miami was the motivator. Everett knew a scholarship to Miami was within his grasp. To make sure he was doing the academic work, Chuck Pagano, then a Miami assistant, phoned Kevin every week to get an update on his grades.

"Junior college is a hard row to hoe," Rieves said. "When you go to a junior college, most Division I schools write you off. But they didn't forget about Kevin."

At Miami, Everett's work ethic enamored him to tight ends coach Mario Cristobal, a man Kevin calls the most influential coach of his career.

But even Cristobal couldn't prepare Everett for what transpired in Buffalo around 2:35 PM on September 9, 2007. That was the day Kevin Everett, up-and-coming tight end for the Buffalo Bills, collapsed near the Denver 20-yard line after making a tackle that his high school coach, Celaya, has watched dozens of times.

"When I see the video footage, it's a matter of inches," he said.

He meant that it was an inch or two away from being a perfect tackle. Instead, Everett's head was down a bit, making him vulnerable to the injury.

"I really didn't see him do anything wrong," Celaya said. "His head was [down] so little. I saw the same type of defensive player I always remember—good balance and good feet and hips. He was so explosive, and it's unbelievable to see him go down like that."

"You never had to worry that Kevin would slack off and wouldn't work."

"It was something freaky, a freak accident," said Philadelphia Eagles linebacker Takeo Spikes, Kevin's former teammate with the Bills. "You see a guy make a tackle like that and he usually gets up, but he caught him (Hixon) in just the right angle and right degree."

The right angle to be paralyzed.

"I watched the whole thing and he never moved," Bills cornerback Terrence McGee said. "I've seen that happen on TV before, but never in real life."

Everett's hit on Hixon became a highly popular YouTube video.

Like drivers who stop to watch the aftermath of a car crash, people were searching the Internet to see what caused doctors to call this a potentially tragic tackle.

CHAPTER 3
NORMALCY TURNS TO TERROR

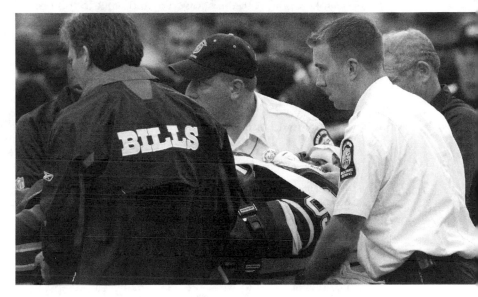

"My first thought was, 'He's not getting up.

Why isn't he getting up?

Why isn't he getting up?!!!"

For Kevin Everett, the morning of September 9, 2007—a day that would change his life—started in typical fashion. The routine included a breakfast that, to most Americans, would seem rather unusual.

Everett woke up at 8:00 AM, showered, and went to the Buffalo Bills' Ralph Wilson Stadium to eat his pregame meal: a few pieces of chicken and some bread.

"I don't like anything too heavy before a game," he said.

After eating, Everett put on his home uniform—the blue one with the white "85" on the jersey—and then had parts of his body taped by the trainer before going onto the field to stretch and do some exercises.

Everett then returned to the locker room with his teammates, sat in front of his locker, and bowed his head.

It was time to put on his game face.

Around the locker room, most of the Buffalo Bills sat with intense stares as they prepared themselves for their season opener against the Denver Broncos. Some of the Bills rode exercise bikes as a form of relaxation, a form of breaking the pregame tension. Some sat by their lockers and listened to music on their iPods; it was a way to calm their nerves, a way to soothe their minds, a way to find tranquility before three hours of organized violence.

Everett closed his eyes and thought about God, thought about things that brought him harmony. "Anything to be peaceful with myself," he said.

The Bills were coming off a 7–9 season, but some talented young players gave them hope for improvement. They believed this would be the year the Bills reached the playoffs for the first time since 1999.

Buffalo had a 2–2 exhibition season. It had been difficult for Kevin because of what was happening to his 11-year-old sister, Davia, back in suburban Houston. Davia was in a diabetic coma for three days and spent two weeks in an intensive-care unit in Texas. Kevin was at the Bills' training camp at St. John Fisher College in Rochester, New York, and all he could do was receive constant medical updates from his mom.

Everett closed his eyes and thought about God, thought about things that brought him harmony.

"It was scary," he said. "That's my baby sister there. It's a terrifying feeling when something happens and you're so far away."

Davia would recover. Soon, it would be Kevin's injury that would spread terror through his family.

❖ ❖ ❖

In contrast to the cloudy, gray sky—it drizzled before the game—the season opener had a promising beginning for the Bills. Roscoe Parrish scored on a 74-yard punt return as Buffalo took a 7–0 advantage with 6 minutes, 17 seconds left in the first quarter.

That gave the Bills a lead they would never relinquish—until the final second. Jason Elam kicked a 42-yard field goal as time expired, silencing the crowd and giving Denver a 15–14 win.

But it was what happened *between* Parrish's punt return and Elam's dramatic kick that became the game's focal point—and forever altered the life of a young man who seemed indestructible.

As Everett lay prone on the artificial turf following his collision with the kick returner, his mother paced back and forth in the sports bar and restaurant in Humble, Texas, where she watched the developments with her husband, Herchel Dugas. The couple had been in the bar for no more than 15 seconds when they saw the 255-pound Everett crumble to the turf.

"My first thought was, 'He's not getting up. Why isn't he getting up? *Why isn't he getting up?!!!*'" Patricia said. "Then I started panicking and started looking at all the televisions because I couldn't believe what I was looking at. I started running around from TV to TV, and the announcers kept talking about it."

With the noise in the bar, Patricia had difficulty hearing what the announcers were saying; she moved closer to the TV set. The announcers didn't ease her concern.

"I was sick with worry," she said. "I was terrified."

She soon would be contacted by Paul Lancaster, the Bills' director of player programs.

Lancaster could not alleviate her fear.

❖ ❖ ❖

Everett and Lancaster had a friendly, easy-going relationship during the three years they knew each other in Buffalo. When they had a conversation, it frequently turned into a playful, trash-talking session about their wardrobes.

Both were impeccable dressers.

Each thought he dressed better than the other.

But on this terrible day, as an ambulance arrived on the field to transport Kevin to the hospital, there was no time to poke fun about wardrobes. There were no jokes. No laughter.

"It's important that you come to Buffalo."

Sitting in the press box at Ralph Wilson Stadium, Lancaster watched Kevin fall face-first to the turf and anxiously waited for a positive sign. When he didn't get one, when he saw Kevin wasn't moving, Lancaster headed to the Bills' locker room to learn the extent of the injury.

In his diverse role as director of player programs, one of Lancaster's duties was to help families cope when their loved one on the Bills was injured. He served as a liaison between the Bills, the injured player, and the injured player's family.

"It's a stressful situation if your child, husband, or brother is hurt, so either I'll call the family or have someone else call," Lancaster said.

He phoned Kevin's mom, Patricia, at the bar in Texas and gave her an update. Kevin was still down, he told her, and was being taken to Millard Fillmore Gates Hospital in Buffalo.

Lancaster could hear the concern, the pain, in Patricia's voice. She wanted to be next to her baby.

"It's important," Lancaster said, "that you come to Buffalo."

Patricia began praying.

"I didn't know how minor his injury was, or how severe it was. I was afraid," she said. "I didn't want anything to happen to my child."

The Bills quickly booked a Houston-to-Buffalo flight for Patricia and Wiande. Patricia called home and told her three daughters that their brother had been injured. Herchell, Kevin's 15-year-old sister, got the phone call, and her reaction left a lasting impression on Kelli, 14.

"Herchell just had a look on her face and I was like, 'What? What's wrong?!'" Kelli said.

The three sisters, including 11-year-old Davia, spent the night sobbing. Patricia told the girls to stay strong. Like their big brother.

"If I need anything, he's always been there for me," Herchell said.

Now it was time for the girls to be there for Kevin.

"I didn't believe it was really happening," Kelli said. "I got sick to my stomach."

The big brother who changed their diapers, played games with them, and took them to the movies had always seemed indestructible on the football field.

"He's the bravest ever. I don't know how to explain it," Davia said.

Wiande spent time consoling the girls as she stayed at Kevin's house that night. She managed to sleep for a few hours before getting ready for the 6:00 AM flight to Buffalo.

"I woke up around 4:00 AM and my eyes were so teary," Wiande wrote in her journal. "I started getting dressed eagerly waiting to get on the plane to see the love of my life. I went downstairs to see if Mrs. Patricia was ready or not and she was still packing. The time is now 5:05 AM and we are still at the house. I looked on the Delta Airlines web page to see if we could check in our bags. No way. I hate being late wherever I go. I was trying to do everything I could to speed up the process and be at the airport on time. Finally, Mrs. Patricia came out of the room with Mr. Herchel behind her, his face dry and drained, with luggage.

"I drove to Bush Intercontinental Airport because Mr. Herchel didn't know his way. We arrived at exactly 5:40 AM. 'We have to get on the flight,' I thought. 'We can't miss this flight.' I helped carry the bags out of the car and hurriedly walked to the ticket counter."

They barely got on board their plane at the Houston airport. When they arrived in Buffalo at around 11:45 AM, they were greeted by Lancaster and Dawn Neufeld, the wife of one of the Bills' players, Ryan Neufeld.

Wiande made some small talk, but she didn't comprehend much of what was being said; her mind was on Kevin.

"I couldn't think of anything but to get to him and see how he was," she said. "Was he okay? How was he feeling? What's going through his head? I tried to stay focused and stay level headed, but…"

It was difficult. The fear of the unknown made it impossible for Wiande to concentrate as she and the group drove to the hospital, afraid of what they might find.

When their car reached the hospital, Dawn Neufeld issued a

warning: "The media is everywhere, trying to get a story and take pictures of the family, so there's security everywhere."

As they got out of the car, the valet hurried to their side and escorted them toward Kevin's intensive-care unit.

Wiande asked God for strength and peace as her group passed a gift shop and coffee booth. In the gift shop, her eyes spotted an angel whose hands were folded in prayer.

Wiande smiled.

"Trust God and know that his grace will endure forever, no matter what the circumstance," she said to herself.

> **"**
>
> *The different feelings of hurt, pain, and heavy burden lay on my heart. I know the pain and the hurt of a mother during this time is beyond words. I turned to Mrs. Patricia. I looked at her body, her eyes, her face. Her outer appearance is so strong, and it still was on our way to Millard Fillmore Hospital, but this time, I saw a different strength. I saw the strength that a mom has to portray for her one and only son, her love, her best friend, her child…and I began to cry.*
>
> —Wiande's journal entry, September 10, 2007
>
> **"**

As Wiande walked down a long hallway, she glanced at Patricia and saw a face filled with fear and helplessness. She squeezed Patricia's hand as the security guard pushed the button that enabled the ICU doors to open slowly.

Wiande and Patricia were not prepared for what they saw when the curtains were drawn: Tubes were seemingly in every part of Kevin's body and his face was badly swollen. He was hooked to a ventilator and in a heavily sedated state.

Standing in disbelief, Wiande dropped her belongings and nearly collapsed before grabbing the railing by Kevin's bed. She cried for Kevin, cried for Mrs. Patricia, cried for the situation.

Patricia's knees buckled, and she felt faint as she looked at her model son.

"This is the worst thing I have ever seen in my whole life," she thought.

It took more than an hour for the two women to compose themselves.

"I looked at his body shaking because of the cooling process started by Dr. Cappuccino," Wiande said, "and I thought, 'I can't even hold him. He's cold and I can't even hold him.'"

Wiande, who took an extended leave of absence from teaching at Spring High to be with Kevin, looked at the just-as-heartbroken woman next to her, Mrs. Patricia. They were together with Kevin, but they felt so alone, so helpless. They shared another long cry.

Dr. Cappuccino, the Buffalo Bills' spinal-injury consultant and the neurosurgeon who helped handle Kevin's surgery, told Wiande and Patricia that this was going to be a long process, but that he was optimistic.

"Kevin," he said, "is a very strong man."

Wiande thanked the doctor for saving Kevin's life and thought to herself about how precious life is...and how it is sometimes taken for granted.

At that point, there was some belief that Kevin would one day be confined to a wheelchair—that is, if he could ever get into a wheelchair. But Wiande looked at the bright side: he was alive.

> "
> *I saw her hurt and her pain, but I knew that at this moment, I would never truly understand what she's going through because I don't have a son. A mother's love is so deep, so strong, and I know that one day I will be able to understand how it feels to have a child and love a child the way Mrs. Patricia loves Kevin.*
>
> —Wiande's journal entry,
> September 10, 2007
> "

"God could have taken him home, but He's not finished with him yet," Wiande wrote in her journal. "He has a purpose in each of our lives, and at that moment, I knew that he had another plan he wants Kevin to take."

While Dr. Cappuccino was upbeat with the family, his meeting with the media had the opposite effect. The day after the injury occurred, Cappuccino told reporters that Kevin Everett was battling for his life, and surgery was performed to fuse the third and fourth vertebrae together.

Cappuccino said Everett had no movement below his shoulders, that he was "not likely" to have a complete recovery, and that the injury remained life-threatening. He added that Everett had the ability to feel in all of his limbs and some leg-muscle movement.

Asked if that made him "cautiously optimistic" that Everett might regain full motion and walk again, Cappuccino was blunt. "By life, I'm an optimist, but as scientist and a clinician, I have to tell you that statistically the chances of that occurring are very small."

He added that Kevin's chances of a full neurological recovery were less than 5 to 10 percent.

The doctor said Kevin remained in a life-threatening situation but that his chances had improved after the surgery. "I want to caution everyone to understand that this is early in the healing phase and this is not a prognostic indicator," he said, "and this young man suffered a potentially lethal and grave injury."

Potentially lethal. The words reverberated around Buffalo, around the NFL, and especially around the Everett household.

After the surgery, Everett was placed on a respirator in the intensive-care unit. Kevin's breathing was compromised when he entered the hospital—it was at about 25 percent of capacity. The respirator was needed because high cervical-spine injuries carry a greater risk of respiration failure if a respirator is not provided. Kevin was also placed in a "deeply sedated, drug-induced state" in hope of providing "every possible mechanism" to alleviate spinal-cord swelling, doctors said.

Cappuccino emphasized that Kevin was not in a coma but in a deeply drug-induced state.

When the surgery was completed, Kevin was given a repeat MRI at about 1:00 AM The MRI showed that the spine was well compressed and that the swelling within the cord was decreased compared to the images that were taken prior to the surgery.

At 5:00 AM, Kevin could move his legs a little—a promising sign—and his temperature was close to normal, at around 98.4 degrees. By 6:30 AM, when examined by Kevin Gibbons—the doctor who performed the surgery with Cappuccino—Kevin's temperature was 99 degrees and seemed to be climbing, even though the hospital staff was using cooling blankets to keep his temperature down.

Earlier, there had been some dialogue among at least three doctors about whether to put Kevin in a hypothermic state to cool his body. The treatment, which has been used in treating strokes, brain injuries, and cardiac arrest, is almost like putting an ice pack on a bruise, doctors said. If you don't use ice, the bruise swells and you have problems.

There are risks involved with the treatment, such as cardiac arrhythmia and major infections—especially when the body temperature drops into the low 90s, Gibbons said.

In Kevin's case, Cappuccino thought the risks were worth it.

When the doctors conferred about using hypothermia, Gibbons called it a "discussion." Cappuccino, who had learned about hypothermia at a seminar held by the Miami Project to Cure Paralysis in December of 2006, said there was "some contention" in those discussions. He was in favor of using hypothermia.

But when Kevin developed a fever, it "helped settle the issue," Gibbons said, "because after the surgery (his body) tried to develop a fairly precipitous rise in temperature. And although we're not all sure cold temperature is good, we know that high temperature is bad in the setting of a neurological injury. So at that point, early Monday morning, a decision was made to cool him down."

Unlike the hypothermia tried in the ambulance, with cold saline solution running into Kevin's bloodstream through a standard IV, this treatment was performed with a machine attached to a special catheter placed inside a large vein. Cold fluid was circulated in and out of the catheter, cooling the blood as it flowed by, but not mixing the cold fluid with his blood.

"It took us a while to get the catheter in," recalled Gibbons, the director of neurosurgery at Millard Fillmore Gates Hospital. It was inserted between 8:00 and 9:00 AM. By 10:30 AM, Kevin's temperature had dropped to 93.8 degrees, Gibbons said.

Would it help Kevin? Would it steer him toward recovery?

❖ ❖ ❖

At the Bills' practice field the day after the injury, Everett's condition—not the Pittsburgh Steelers, Buffalo's next opponent— was foremost on the players' minds.

"It seems like every couple of seconds that go by, it's always popping into your head," said J.P. Losman, the Bills' quarterback. "Going through a walk-through, we're looking for him, wanting to hear his voice."

Everett's locker was undisturbed; a team schedule and his cleats rested atop a stool.

"It's very surreal," said an emotional Brian Moorman, the Bills' punter. "I think it's probably the hardest thing I'll ever have to go through as an individual, just watching him go through something like that. It's a close team, probably the closest team I've ever been on since I've been in Buffalo, and when you see that happen, it's really tough."

"We honor ourselves by our work, and we honor Kevin by moving forward and working while never forgetting Kevin and never getting him out of our thoughts and prayers," said Dick Jauron, Buffalo's head coach.

The day after the injury, Bills tight end Matt Murphy visited Everett at the hospital. Kevin was in a deeply sedated state and couldn't communicate with anyone.

"It was hard to see him like that," said Murphy, a five-year veteran who had been released by the Bills but was added to the roster to replace Everett. "Someone you know who's such a great athlete...big and strong. But I know he's a fighter."

"Football is just a game. Football is not important now."

Someone at the hospital told Murphy that Kevin could hear his words.

"I just tried to tell him we're all here for him and care about him and love him," Murphy said. "I told him he's one of the toughest guys I know, and if there's anyone who can pull through it, I know he can. And no matter what was said about his condition, that we're all pulling hard for him, too. I told him I think he'll get through this."

Lancaster, the Bills' executive who used to exchange good-natured barbs with Kevin about their wardrobes, was devastated by Kevin's appearance when he entered the hospital room. Lancaster had heard Cappuccino's grim news conference and knew Kevin would likely remain paralyzed. But as he saw his friend lying in bed, connected to life support, he wondered if Kevin would survive.

"You hear the reports on him and then when you walk in and actually see him, your thoughts turn to the worst. Mine did," Lancaster said. "I was not very comfortable seeing him like that because I know Kevin as a vibrant, active guy."

Moorman, one of the many Bills to visit Kevin at the hospital, became emotional when he saw his teammate and friend hooked to a respirator and in a sedated state.

"All you could do was wonder what was going through his head, because he couldn't tell you," said Moorman, who was joined by his wife, Amber, at Kevin's bedside.

Moorman and his wife were distraught. They left the Buffalo hospital and drove 30 minutes to their home, never saying a word during the entire trip.

Bills tight end Robert Royal returned from a hospital visit and also seemed visibly shaken.

"Football is just a game," he said. "Football is not important now."

In the hospital, Patricia stroked Kevin's arm. Even though he was unable to speak because of a tube in his mouth, he managed to communicate by pursing his lips together. He needed a kiss.

"He wanted some sugar," Patricia said. "I felt much better then."

As Patricia watched Kevin drift back to sleep, she daydreamed back to happier times in his life. There was Kevin taking his first steps as Patricia and her dad cheered loudly; there was Kevin climbing atop his first bike—the

"I just tried to tell him we're all here for him and care about him and love him."

one Patricia's dad bought him for Christmas—and never once taking a spill; there was Kevin making his first career touchdown catch as a member of the Miami Hurricanes, with Patricia and her three daughters screaming and hugging each other as they watched the play unfold on TV.

Then she imagined Kevin reaching another milestone: walking. Again. Staying positive was the only way to get through this ordeal, the only way to stay sane.

Lying in his hospital bed, Kevin gave himself a pep talk. "I just kept saying to myself that this is a minor injury, that it's not that serious," he said. "I would not let it set in that this was something major that happened to me. That's one of the things that kept me motivated."

There were some fleeting moments, however, when fear filled him. Fear that he would never walk again. Fear that, if he did regain the use of his legs, he would walk with a significant limp. Or worse.

When those thoughts developed, Kevin quickly changed the channel in his head. He needed to stay positive, needed to stay focused as he tried to recover from an injury that rarely occurs, especially on the professional level.

From 1977 to 2006, the National Center for Catastrophic Sport Injury Research at the University of North Carolina had documented 269 "catastrophic" injuries to the cervical cord among football players. Most of those cases—222—involved junior high and high school players.

In that 30-season span, only nine of the injuries were suffered by pros, including the one suffered by the Detroit Lions' Mike Utley.

Two days after Everett's injury, Utley made a heartfelt video for Kevin. Utley, a former Lions guard, was paralyzed below the chest in a 1991 game. He fractured the sixth and seventh cervical vertebrae while pass blocking against the Los Angeles Rams.

Though a paraplegic, Utley kayaks, scuba dives, skydives, and pedals a hand cycle, among other activities.

When he watched Everett go down on September 9, Utley's mind raced back to 1991: "Here we go again," he thought.

"We have a young man who's a great athlete, and now we have to get him to a place where he'll have the best chance to win," Utley said. "He got to the NFL through hard work. He knows how to work hard. He's going to need that to get better. If there's a will, there's a way. If there's a way, there's a chance to win."

FINDING A HOME IN MIAMI

CHAPTER 4

"His biggest attribute," Cristobal said, "is his pride. He's a guy who,
at all costs, wanted to be the best
and put in the extra time in the film room
and the weight room, or went out early at practice to catch
extra balls. He was a perfectionist."

Long before his life was turned upside down by a tackle that ended his promising football career, Kevin Everett was a highly sought-after high school player who had narrowed his collegiate choices to Miami, Auburn, and Florida.

Truth be told, Auburn and Florida were far behind his number one choice, Miami. Kevin had always been enamored by Miami's wide-open offense...and the fact Michael Irvin was a star wide receiver for the Hurricanes.

"I was a big Michael Irvin fan and he played for the Cowboys, and I was a Cowboy fan," Kevin said, "so when I found out he played for the Hurricanes, it was like, 'Wow.'"

Ironically, Everett was the anti-Irvin in the way he played. He didn't do anything to resemble the flamboyant nature of Irvin. Everett's high school coach said Kevin politely handed the ball to the referee after scoring a touchdown—a practice seldom displayed by the show-boating Irvin.

Before he could make an impact at the University of Miami, Everett had to make a stop at a Texas junior college.

At Kilgore, Everett was a two-time All-Southwest Junior College tight end, and he earned the necessary grades to transfer to Miami.

Kilgore's coach recalled Everett as a quiet person who was serious about his education and focused on getting to Miami.

"He didn't party or do any of those kind of things, and never got in any trouble, which is unusual at a junior college," said Jimmy Rieves, Kevin's coach at Kilgore. "He was very unassuming."

When he got to Miami, a national powerhouse that was coached by Larry Coker, Everett felt at home.

Mario Cristobal was the main reason.

Cristobal coached the tight ends. He was a people person, and he and Everett quickly developed a bond, hanging out and forming a close-knit relationship that was more player-player than coach-player.

"He was the best coach I ever had," Kevin said. "He was hard on me and wouldn't let me settle for less; he wanted to make sure I reached my full potential. He cared about you, on and off the field, and called me every day. I stayed out of a lot of trouble because of him, because I would be hanging out with him."

Cristobal pushed hard. Kevin wanted to be pushed hard. That, in a nutshell, is why they became inseparable. They were from the same mold.

"He means the world to me," said Cristobal, now the 37-year-old head coach at Florida International. "He affected my life in a big-time way and I love him. He always had a dream to go to Miami and he took the hard road to get there. He went to Kilgore—and that's not a road you dream of taking—and got it done."

Cristobal, whose high-energy, rapid-fire delivery is in direct contrast to Everett's laid-back personality, was good at what he did. While coaching at Rutgers, he mainly coached the tight ends and offensive linemen, and he helped pave the way for the Scarlet Knights' turnaround. One of his prize pupils was tight end L.J. Smith, the Philadelphia Eagles' second-round selection in the 2003 NFL Draft.

When he became a Miami assistant in 2004, Everett was a senior. The two formed a unique bond, going out to dinner, talking football at the Hurricanes' facility, or watching game film long after practice had ended.

"A lot of coaches are just there for a paycheck and don't try to have a relationship. I find that odd," said Everett, adding that he may get into coaching down the road. "He built relationships with people. He let you know when you're doing something wrong, but he also let you know when you did something good. Some coaches just fuss and cuss and only let you know when you're doing something wrong. That eats at you. I've had coaches from both sides.

"I think coaching should bring out the best in players, and that's what Mario did."

Miami was a school deep in tight-end tradition, and Cristobal wanted Everett to be part of that legacy. The Hurricanes' previous three starting tight ends were Bubba Franks, Jeremy Shockey, and Kellen Winslow Jr., all of whom were chosen in the top half of the first round of the NFL Draft.

Cristobal thought Everett belonged with that select company.

During a practice late in Kevin's junior year, he and Winslow were jawing about which one was the faster tight end—at least that's how one coach remembers it. Around Miami, Cristobal said, it has become known as "one of the greatest days in Miami practice history. They were just two guys who loved to compete."

"His makeup is unbelievable. You want to go to war with a guy like that."

Toward the end of practice, the players surrounded the field; they clapped and hollered as the two behemoths with great speed lined up for a 40-yard dash.

Advantage, Everett.

"Kevin," Cristobal said, "was a 250-pounder who ran like a 150-pounder."

Actually, Kevin claimed he didn't want to race Winslow. "To me, it was no big deal who was the fastest," Everett said. "But the team and the coaches were challenging us. Everybody was saying he (Winslow) was the fastest tight end in the country. And Coach (Rob) Chudzinski was calling us out on it."

Everett said he "smoked" Winslow. "It was real easy," he said, trying to keep a straight face.

Cristobal was always disappointed that he only coached Kevin for one season.

"I wish I could have had him for four years, or even two years," Cristobal said.

As a senior, Everett caught 23 passes for 310 yards and was a solid blocker. Outsiders could see Kevin's size, strength, and speed, but those weren't his best qualities, Cristobal said.

Miami was a school deep in tight-end tradition, and Cristobal wanted Everett to be part of that legacy.

"His biggest attribute," Cristobal said, "is his pride. He's a guy who, at all costs, wanted to be the best and put in the extra time in the film room and the weight room, or went out early at practice to catch extra balls. He was a perfectionist. I've been around Shockey and L.J. Smith and him...and they're in the same group."

No one outworked Everett, Cristobal said.

"Even in the summertime, he'd ask me to go out and set up the machine so he'd have balls thrown to him all afternoon. Some people talk about working hard; this guy is a freaking maniac about it. He attacks the game and wants to become a better player. Attacks it with a passion. He went from 225 to 252 pounds and his power-clean went to 385. Even a 330-pound lineman couldn't touch what he could.

"His makeup is unbelievable. You want to go to war with a guy like that."

Everett ran crisp pass routes and developed into a dominating blocker. In fact, when Cristobal shows his Florida International players instructional films on those two areas, "most of the tapes are of Kevin Everett," the coach said.

Cristobal gets "excited and fired up" when he talks about Everett as a player. He said there's "no question in my mind" Everett was on the verge of becoming a top-flight NFL tight end. "He's in the same mold of L.J. (Smith) and Shockey; their physical qualities are very similar," he said. "He and L.J. have about the same speed, but Kevin's a little faster than Shockey."

That, of course, was before the devastating spinal injury.

❖❖❖

Besides establishing a special friendship with Cristobal and many others associated with the Hurricanes' football program, there was another bonus about attending the University of Miami.

It brought Kevin together with Wiande Moore.

Wiande came from a close-knit, high-achieving family of three girls and two boys who lived in Spring, Texas, located about a 75-minute drive from Kevin's roots in Port Arthur. The two didn't meet each other until they attended Miami.

It wasn't her Texas roots that drew Kevin to Wiande. It was her stunning looks and her effervescent personality.

"You know, that was one of the key things," said Kevin, referring to Wiande's beauty. "But just getting to know her and see what's on her mind and what was going on with her. Just stuff like that attracted me to her."

It wasn't one thing. It was lots of things. Her laugh. Her infectious smile. Her spirituality. It was the way she was devoted to her family, the way she was loyal to her friends. Immensely.

They met at the University of Miami athletic center, where both of them used to train. "We were stretching outside before we went to work out," Wiande said.

They were comfortable with each other, and the conversation came easily.

"After the first day we met, we started hanging out, just spending every day together," Kevin said. "Just talking and getting to know each other, basically."

Wiande had been through some bad relationships. This would

be different, she thought. Kevin was unlike the other guys she had dated.

"He was more of a laid-back guy—and he still is," she said. "But at the same time, he is caring and likes to have fun; he knows when to have fun and when to be serious. I like that about him."

She phoned her sister Wayetu (pronounced Why-ETT-to) and gave her the good news about meeting Kevin.

Wayetu, who was attending New York University at the time, and Wiande had been inseparable growing up in Texas. They would make up silly dances to songs performed by Brian Mc-Knight, Boyz II Men, and SWV. They would go to the movies with friends, or play H-O-R-S-E on the basketball court in their front yard.

When Wiande ran in sprint and long distance events for Spring High's track team, Wayetu was one of her biggest fans.

"In high school, people would go to her track meets to see her because she ran with such ease," Wayetu said, proudly. "When you say 'track,' people don't get excited, but she made it look so easy that people would go watch. She made it to states as a freshman and was always the team's MVP."

Wiande won the 100-meter dash in a school record 11.71 seconds. She also excelled in relays and eventually earned a track scholarship to Miami. There, though, she no longer dominated meets. Not at first, anyway.

"She was used to being the best," Wayetu said, "but when you go to a D-I school, *everybody* on the team is great and you have to find your way."

By the end of her senior year, she was a four-time All-American, winning three of the honors as a senior—two during the NCAA outdoor season (4x100-meter relay and 4x400 relay) and one during the indoor season (lead leg of the 4x400 relay).

Wiande had managed to have the same success on the national level that she had at Spring High, where she was the MVP during each of her four seasons.

The reputation Wiande built in high school probably played a role in younger sister Wayetu earning a varsity track spot as a Spring freshman.

"I guess they thought I was fast because I was her sister," she said.

In one of the first races of her high-school career, "they had me run the 400, and I fainted at the finish line and went to the hospital," said Wayetu, adding that tests showed she was hyper-glycemic and didn't have enough proteins and nutrients in her system. "That became a running joke about my track career. I was more of a tennis and dance-team girl."

Besides Wiande, 24, and Wayetu, 22, the family includes their sister, Kula, 21, a budding artist who is finishing her final year at Baylor. (Wayetu, a journalism major, is in her senior year at Howard and plans to attend Columbia to study screenwriting.) They have two athletic brothers, Gus Jr., 17, and David, 15, each of whom are taking advanced classes at the Texas high school where Wiande teaches. "When they run out of lunch money, I see them," Wiande said.

The siblings' father, Gus Sr., is an engineer, and their mother, Mamawa, is a teacher who has aspirations of opening her own school. "My mom loves kids," Wayetu said. "She kids that when we all move out, she's going to adopt."

"We come from a family of educators and engineers and we're looking to help other people," Wayetu said. "Wiande had feelers to turn pro in track, but she wanted to do other things. She always wanted to teach, and she just decided that (track at Miami) is as far as she would go."

❖ ❖ ❖

Wayetu heard the excitement in Wiande's voice the night she first described Kevin. She listened and let her sister express her joy. Deep down, however, she wondered if her sister was doing the right thing.

Even though she was two years younger than Wiande, Wayetu played the part of protective big sister. She didn't want to see her sister get hurt again.

"She had a line of bad relationships," Wayetu said. "She was always very loyal and took it seriously—and not all guys in college have that on their mind. She told me about Kevin and I said, 'Cool.' But I worried because she was just in a string of bad relationships and I didn't want her to have another one."

The fact that Kevin was a football player bothered Wayetu.

"College athletes are not known as faithful men," she said. "I just wanted to make sure she was on the right path."

After a while, Kevin began to grow on the overprotective sister.

"In time, after I got to know Kevin, I realized this was something they both believed in," Wayetu said of the relationship. "They have some issues, like everyone else, but at the end of the day, what they have is true."

❖ ❖ ❖

During his junior year at Miami, Kevin Everett met another person who would become an important part of his life: Eric Armstead.

As a partner with E.O. Sports Management in Houston, one of Armstead's duties was to recruit promising college football players for the agency. Armstead would scour Mel Kiper's college recruiting reports—and other sources that rated players—to get a feel for the top prospects. Armstead was a workaholic, and it wasn't unusual for him to put in a 16-hour day.

Armstead was intrigued by reports he had been reading about Everett as a junior college player. Scouts were calling him the nation's top junior college tight end. The intrigue grew when he noticed Everett was from Port Arthur, Texas, the same city where Armstead's wife had grown up.

"I saw he was going to Miami and that was unusual for someone who was from Texas," Armstead said. "If you're from Texas, you usually go to Texas or Oklahoma or Texas A&M. I got Kevin's number and started calling him."

Drew Rosenhaus and some of the other big-time agents were also recruiting Everett, Armstead said. But Armstead thought his Texas roots—he lived in Houston, not far from Port Arthur—might help him one day sign Everett as a client.

During Everett's junior season at Miami, Armstead would phone the tight end three times a week. They would talk about Miami's upcoming game, about Kevin's health, and his family. Anything to establish a rapport.

Armstead told Everett he thought he would be a high draft selection after his senior year and that his firm wanted to represent him one day.

"We're from Texas, like you," Armstead would remind him.

After dozens of phone calls, Armstead finally got to meet Kevin when he returned to Texas during his winter semester break of his junior year. Armstead had met Kevin's biological dad through his sister-in-law. "His dad was working for a janitorial service in Beaumont, and my sister-in-law was the health director there," Armstead said.

Armstead thought it was the connection he needed, one that would pave the way for eventually signing Kevin as a client.

"I'm thinking Kevin and his dad are real close," Armstead said, "and then I talk to Kevin one day and he said, 'My dad and I don't really talk much.' I thought, 'Oh, I'm barking up the wrong tree here.'"

Armstead went to Plan B and met with Kevin's mom, Patricia

Dugas, at her apartment in the Joe Louis Projects, located in a poor section of Port Arthur. Armstead and Patricia talked for a while, and later that day they met Kevin at his cousin's house in Port Arthur.

"It was the first time we met in person," Armstead said. "We watched a little TV, and had some small talk." Patricia had to excuse herself; she kissed Kevin goodbye and hurried over to the local Wal-Mart, where she worked as a cashier. Kevin and Armstead continued talking.

"I told him that next year was going to be a big year for him and that we wanted to represent him," Armstead said. "I told him we were there for him."

At the time, little did anyone know that Kevin and Armstead would develop much more than a player-client relationship.

They would develop a friendship that had lasting power.

"We're real tight," Kevin said. "We do everything together—go out to get something to eat, take a trip, or just call each other up and hang out."

❖ ❖ ❖

After his senior season at Miami, Everett thought he had a chance to be selected late in the first round or perhaps early in the second round of the 2005 NFL Draft. But his stock slipped when he tore ligaments in his left shoulder in Miami's season finale, requiring him to have surgery. Everett attended the Scouting Combine but was unable to work out or do any drills because his shoulder was still recovering.

The Bills selected him in the third round with the draft's 86th overall pick.

"Because I didn't have a solid workout, something to go off of at the Combine, I went lower than I expected," Everett said. "I was disappointed. I was kind of upset about it, but I knew I had to accept it."

He had been hoping to be selected by the Dallas Cowboys. "I even talked to them before the draft more than any other team, but…"

Everett was Buffalo-bound. He embraced the idea. He was given a four-year contract for a little more than $2.1 million. However, only a portion of that contract—a $600,000 signing bonus—was guaranteed.

Kevin Everett was headed to the NFL, many years removed from not being permitted to play peewee football because he was too big.

Tom Modrak, Buffalo's director of college scouting, thought he had selected a third-round steal. He had Kevin listed as one of the draft's best tight ends.

"He had so much going for him," Modrak said.

In addition to his strength, Everett displayed uncommonly good speed for a tight end. "You want a tight end who can be a deep threat, as well as someone who can catch the ball underneath," Modrak said. "Kevin could do both. And he blocked well in college, but he was even better when he got to our place because he got stronger and more physically mature."

In Buffalo, Everett's road to stardom was somewhat bumpy. He suffered a season-ending torn anterior-cruciate ligament in his left knee during his first pro training camp. "To his credit, he never backed away from hard work," Modrak said. "If he needed to do rehab work, he did it. If he needed to get to the field early to get in extra work, he was there early. He wasn't a woe-is-me type."

In 2006, his second season with the Bills, he was used sparingly but was making slow, steady progress. He cracked the starting lineup in five of 16 games.

"He was a perfectionist," said Philadelphia Eagles linebacker Takeo Spikes, who was one of Everett's teammates during his first two seasons in Buffalo. He called Everett "a hard-working guy

A young Kevin Everett, when he was a two-way starter (at both offensive and defensive end) for Port Arthur (Texas) Thomas Jefferson High School.

Kevin and his mom, Patricia Dugas, on his high school graduation day. Patricia remains a very important person in Kevin's life.

Kevin spent two years at Kilgore (Texas) Junior College, twice earning all-Southwest Junior College Conference honors, graduating in just 1½ years, and proving that he was ready to make the jump to Division I football.

In 2003 Kevin signed on to play for the University of Miami, a school with a rich tradition of sending tight ends to the NFL.

Kevin strides into the end zone with a touchdown during a Miami home game.

NFL scouts regarded Kevin as a "complete" tight end—a strong blocker as well as a gifted receiver.

Kevin proudly displays a Miami Everett/88 jersey after signing to play for the college football powerhouse, though he ended up wearing number 84 while a member of the Hurricanes.

Kevin pulls in a pass in a 2004 game against Louisville.

Kevin warms up prior to a game at the Orange Bowl in Miami in 2004.

In a scene eerily reminiscent of what would take place in Buffalo three years later, Kevin lies in pain on the turf after injuring his shoulder in 2004 against Virginia Tech. The injury, which ended Kevin's senior season at Miami, required surgery and hurt his prospects as an NFL draft choice.

Kevin keeps cool on the sideline during a game against Wake Forest at the Orange Bowl in Miami.

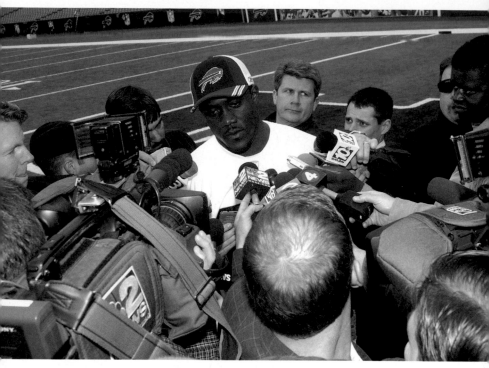

Shortly after being drafted by the Bills in the third round of the 2005 draft, Kevin participated in his first NFL minicamp in Buffalo, and met the press.

Just a few weeks prior to his injury, Kevin played a preseason game against the Atlanta Falcons.

Kevin made a name for himself on special teams during the 2006 season. Here he pressures Hunter Smith, punter for the Indianapolis Colts.

Kevin runs with the ball after making a catch against the Chicago Bears at Soldier Field in Chicago in 2006.

During his brief NFL career, Kevin developed a reputation as a tough player and a great contributor on special teams.

who had an attention to detail, and he wanted everything on the field to be perfect. He was a tight end who could stretch the field (with his speed) and had big-play ability."

Steve Fairchild was named Buffalo's offensive coordinator in Everett's second year, so it was a season to learn a new system.

"His progress was slowed by a change in offensive coordinators," Modrak said. "He was coming off the knee injury one year and the confidence wasn't there, and then he had new terminology to learn (the next year), but he was making it. He was really making strides. He was really just starting to bloom and turn heads."

"You want a tight end who can be a deep threat, as well as someone who can catch the ball underneath. Kevin could do both."

Finally healthy in training camp in 2007, Everett figured to get lots of playing time and be more involved in the Bills' offense. It was going to be the year he made an impact.

"You could clearly see it," Bills coach Dick Jauron said of Everett's improvement. "He was playing a lot more snaps. He was featured. Kevin has done a terrific job."

Modrak said Everett was developing into a tight end with similar traits as L.J. Smith, the Philadelphia Eagles' productive tight end. Kevin was a guy "who could run and beat cover-two (where two safeties play deep) and catch the ball well, and he was not just an okay blocker. He was a strong blocker, so he had the best of both worlds. Was he at the top of his game in both? No. He had room for improvement, but he was good in both. His time would have gone up this year and he would have been on his way."

Besides the increased playing duties, Kevin was also becoming a leader in the locker room. He took pride in staying around the locker room longer and getting to know his teammates and what made them tick. He wasn't just there to collect a paycheck. He was there to build relationships that would last beyond football.

"A wonderful teammate," is how Bills tight end Robert Royal described Everett. "Very determined and hard-working, and he definitely tried to do things the right way."

"He was a guy you wanted to be around," Modrak said.

"You could see him making progress as a player and as a person."

Buffalo wide receiver Roscoe Parrish probably knows Everett better than any other player, having played with him at Miami and with the Bills. When they played at Miami, they kidded about how great it would be if they played on the same team—never dreaming they would be selected in consecutive rounds by the Bills in the 2005 NFL Draft. Parrish was chosen in the second round, Everett in the third.

"We were close friends in Miami and we got closer in Buffalo," Parrish said.

They often hung out together in the Buffalo area, going to restaurants, talking trash as they competed on one of the region's bowling lanes, or shooting hoops at Dave & Busters, an action-packed restaurant and bar featuring arcade games and video screens with Buffalo sporting events.

That was Kevin's idea of a good time—playing video games or going bowling. He wasn't a partier, wasn't into the club scene.

"K was a guy who always stood out," Parrish said. "When you meet him, he's a very respectable guy. He talks to everyone and he's someone with a lot of energy. He's a guy you wanted to build around and have on your team."

He was a guy who would almost always stay after practice to

run extra routes with his position coach or catch extra balls from a pass-throwing machine.

"You could see him making progress as a player and as a person," said Royal, another of Kevin's many good friends. "He was fun to be around, a spirited person and guys liked to be around him. He's not the kind of guy to start a conversation. He's kind of quiet, but he's noticeable with his presence. And when you get to know him, he's a jokester."

When Kevin first meets you, he's a little guarded, said Paul Lancaster, a Bills' executive. "But once you get with him and he gets to know you, he shows you the love."

His competitive nature is legendary.

Wiande could see that when she played Scrabble or checkers with Kevin. Royal could see it when he worked out with Kevin in the weight room.

"He competes in *everything*," Royal said with a smile. "In the weight room, we talk a lot of trash. He'll show off and do a whole bunch of weights and get you to compete. That's him. Always competing. I love that about him, that true competitive spirit."

That drive helped Everett become a standout in high school and college and had him climbing the ladder toward success in the NFL.

"But the moons didn't line up that day," Modrak said, referring to September 9, the fateful afternoon when Everett was injured.

CHAPTER 5

FROM BUFFALO, WITH LOVE

"We were amazed by all the support of the

hospital staff and the people.

They couldn't do enough for all of us."

With Kevin heavily sedated and on a respirator, Wiande and Patricia tried to get some sleep at a nearby hotel. Soon they would keep an around-the-clock vigil at the hospital.

It was Tuesday, two days after the injury, and Wiande and Patricia were groggy from taking sleeping pills the night before.

"I had to wake up to reality and do what I could," Wiande said.

They arrived at the hospital and were again escorted to the ICU by security guards. The hospital had arranged a lounge room for the Everett family, and it was filled with flowers—including an arrangement of yellow tulips sent by Whoopi Goldberg—boxes of get-well cards, and signs from people who were wishing Kevin a full recovery. The room was also stocked with food and drinks for Kevin's family, and folks from all around the country—especially Port Arthur, Texas, and Buffalo—were calling or sending "get well" e-mails.

"We were amazed by all the support of the hospital staff and the people," Wiande said. "They couldn't do enough for all of us."

Wiande took a deep breath before walking into Kevin's ICU room.

She was excited about what she saw.

Kevin was able to open and close his eyes. Wiande was told he could hear, so she started to talk to Kevin. With her voice quivering, she sweetly sang "Still in Love" by Brian McKnight. Kevin had a tube in his mouth, and he stared at Wiande.

He didn't respond to the song.

"I've got to be strong. I've got to be strong," Wiande repeated to herself.

Later that day, Wiande and Patricia went back to the hotel for some rest. They were flabbergasted by the items the Buffalo Bills' Women's Association, composed of the players' wives and girlfriends, had sent: boxes of food and snacks, magazines, books, and almost anything imaginable.

Paul Lancaster, the Bills' director of player programs, and Gretchen Geitter, who was the team's executive director of community relations, always seemed to be at the hospital to assist the family. Bills president Ralph Wilson, a strong supporter of the Miami Project to Cure Paralysis, had told Lancaster that Kevin was the team's top concern.

"Do whatever you need to do," Wilson said to Lancaster.

The Bills' organization was in rally mode.

Wiande returned numerous phone calls and text messages. In her journal that night, she wrote about the love and support Kevin and the family had been receiving.

In a press release issued by the Bills, Kevin's mom thanked fans for their prayers and the hospital staff and Buffalo organization for their support "during this difficult and challenging time. I would ask for everyone to continue to keep Kevin in their prayers."

The prayers were seemingly answered. Andrew Cappuccino, one of the doctors who performed the spinal surgery on Everett and who one day earlier had said a recovery was highly unlikely, gave a stunning account to a Buffalo TV station: Kevin had voluntary movement of his arms and legs and, as a result, Cappuccino was optimistic he would walk again.

"We may be witnessing a minor miracle," Cappuccino said.

"I don't know if I would call it a miracle," said Dr. Barth Green, chairman of the department of neurological surgery at the University of Miami school of medicine. "I would call it a spectacular example of what people can do. To me, it's like putting the first man on the moon or splitting the atom. We've shown that, if the right treatment is given to people who have a catastrophic injury, they could walk away from it."

One of the keys, Green said, was the quick action by Cappuccino to run an ice-cold saline solution through Everett's system in the ambulance.

The treatment attempts to nudge the body into a state of hypothermia—a step aimed at limiting a string of events in the body that can lead to further spinal-cord damage after the injury.

Hypothermia was also used after Kevin's surgery. Kevin Gibbons, one of the neurosurgeons at Millard Fillmore Gates Hospital who operated on Everett, said his medical team had decided to use the cooling process when Kevin's body temperature rose dramatically.

Kevin's journey to recovery was far from over.

In a press conference at the hospital, he made the decision sound so simple: "Although we are not sure that cold temperature is good, we know high temperature is bad in a neurological injury," Gibbons said.

Cappuccino later said there was a heated debate among doctors as to whether to use the hypothermia. Cappuccino was in favor of the method; some other doctors weren't.

Despite the positive developments, spinal-cord experts believed the next 24 hours would be critical in determining the extent of Everett's injury. Kevin's movement was a major step, but some medical experts warned that it might only be a spasm.

❖ ❖ ❖

When Wiande awoke and headed to the hospital the next day, she was anxious to see if any of the tubes had been removed from Kevin's body. She passed a marquee at a local high school that said, "Please Join Us in Praying for Kevin Everett."

As Wiande and Patricia got to the hospital, a media swarm had gathered outside. The hospital staff helped the two women get into the hospital unnoticed, and they quickly walked to Kevin's room.

Wiande was greeted by a gift.

"The biggest smile I have ever seen," she said.

The smile was Kevin's. The Kevin who belonged to her and Mrs. Patricia.

"Hey, baby!! I love you!!" Wiande said.

"Hey, my sweet potato," Patricia said, tears streaking down her cheeks. "I love you, baby!"

Kevin's journey to recovery was far from over. In fact, it was still in the earliest stages. But this was a moment that the trio would always cherish—a moment that told them life might one day return to normal.

"For the first time on this trip, I saw Mrs. Patricia at ease a little. She was still in hurt and pain, but just knowing that Kevin was up and acknowledged who we were was the best thing that could ever happen to us," Wiande wrote in her journal.

Wiande and Patricia stayed by Kevin's side and talked and talked and talked. He still couldn't talk because of a breathing tube that was in his mouth, but he could communicate with a board that had symbols and letters printed on it.

Even with the board, the communication process wasn't easy. "We were all frustrated at times," Wiande said, "but we finally got a clear understanding of how to use it."

Kevin's mom left the room to talk with some Buffalo Bills executives and some hospital workers.

Wiande stayed by Kevin's side, kissing him and caressing his face. She then asked someone from the hospital to give her more help with the communication board.

Kevin, his voice garbled by the breathing tube, got out his first words. "I love you," he said.

For one of the few times since Kevin's injury, Wiande started to feel some peace.

In her journal, Wiande's words resonated with deep affection:

"I thought about us, about our life together. I visualized him walking and chasing me around the house like he always does. I visualized my baby away from the hospital, away from the pain and away from feeling helpless and dependent. But then reality hit and I was standing next to Kevin with a smile on my face. He looked at me for strength. He looked at me in my eyes and told me with tubes in his mouth, 'I'm yours.'"

❖ ❖ ❖

Wiande decided to stay overnight at the Buffalo hospital. Now that Kevin was able to open his eyes and communicate, she couldn't sleep unless she was near him. She slept on a recliner next to Kevin's bed.

Later in the day, she attended a Bible-study session. She shared Kevin's circumstances with everyone.

"Though it seems hard and though we want to ask questions," she wrote in her journal, God says, 'Just trust me.'"

"Every day is good news. Every day, he gets better."

As the week progressed, Kevin continued to get letters, flowers, and food from all over the world. On Thursday—four days after he sustained the injury—Kevin still had a tube in his mouth.

"It's difficult to communicate with him, but he has good spirits and his attitude is really positive," Wiande said.

Dr. Cappuccino spoke to Wiande and Patricia about removing some tubes in the near future. Cappuccino and Dr. John Marzo, the Bills' medical director, said they were encouraged by Kevin's progress. Kevin had moved his legs and toes during the day, but he was still cold and he still continued to have spasms, perhaps associated with the hypothermia.

When the doctors left, Wiande stayed in the room. Patricia continued to talk to people from the Bills' organization—more than 50 were there that day. Running back Anthony Thomas, Kevin's best friend on the team, and tight end Ryan Neufeld were among the Bills who were by the tight end's side.

"Every day is good news. Every day, he gets better," Wiande told them.

Later that day, she and Patricia went to the Bills' practice and thanked the team for its support. Then it was back to the hospital, back to encourage Kevin.

Kevin was restless during the night. He kept coughing and spitting and didn't get much sleep. Wiande assisted him and slept in a recliner next to him. She thought about how she missed cuddling in bed with Kevin to watch a movie or to just hold each other.

Wiande found herself getting weaker and weaker. She cried herself to sleep.

❖ ❖ ❖

Wiande and Patricia were virtually living at Millard Fillmore Gates Hospital. They would return briefly to their hotel to shower, then they would head back to the hospital. Friends were telling them to take a break and go to a restaurant, but it was difficult to leave the man they both loved.

"It was so hard to leave because every time I left the room, I felt guilty and I thought about him, my baby, my heart. I thought about how he was feeling and asked myself questions," Wiande wrote in her journal. "But deep down, I knew that everything would be OK."

On this day, Wiande and Patricia were joined at the hospital by Kevin's biological father. Outside the hospital, a huge "Get Well" sign was displayed from a Buffalo radio station. Beneath it were flowers, teddy bears, and gifts.

Wiande was overwhelmed and began crying.

She wrote the feelings in her journal:

"I thought about Kevin. I thought about our long conversations, about how one day everyone's going to know his name. But I knew when we spoke of this, we never imagined it would be this way. We never thought that everyone would know his name due to a spinal-cord injury, but then again, no one knows their future. We make plans to do things and we make goals about dreams that we might not ever achieve or reach, but at the same time, we have to dream and be goal-oriented because if we aren't, then we wouldn't be great entrepreneurs, athletes, doctors, or teachers. The wind blew on my face as I stood there in deep thought, praying for peace and strength as I prepared to go upstairs to the ICU."

At a press conference, doctors explained that Kevin had regained some movement in his legs, a little in his arms, and none in his hands. They said they didn't expect Kevin to walk soon but were guardedly optimistic that he might be able to someday. No further surgeries were planned, but they were possible if complications arose, they said.

Gibbons called it "a chronic life-threatening state."

Dr. Gibbons said Kevin had made "significant progress" and was taken off the breathing tube but added that "no one should think the function in his legs is normal. Not even close. He has no function in his hands.... If you asked me if he would walk again, I wouldn't bet against it. But he has a long way to go."

Dr. Cappuccino said he was "cautiously, slightly more optimistic" about Kevin's chances of ever walking.

"We still are looking at a many more weeks to months scenario," Cappuccino said. "Walking out of this hospital is not a very realistic goal, but walking may be.... My hope is that he will walk again, but I can only base my opinions each day on the clinical evaluation of the patient."

Gibbons said Kevin was in a quadriplegic state after the injury, but the next day he was able to push his knees together on command. He was then placed under sedation, but when the sedation was lifted, Kevin could wiggle his toes, move his ankles slightly, and kick out his lower leg with his knees elevated, the doctor explained.

Kevin was awake and alert and was being fed through a tube. Doctors remained wary of potentially fatal blood clots, infection, gastrointestinal bleeding, and pulmonary problems.

Gibbons called it "a chronic life-threatening state."

The doctor seemed cautiously optimistic four days after the surgery, which was the same day Kevin received a visit from NFL Commissioner Roger Goodell.

Patricia Dugas, Kevin's mom, seemed more upbeat than the doctors.

"He has determination I've never seen; he's strong in his mind," she said. "Kevin is a faithful and God-loving person, and that's what's helping him; he's holding onto his faith that he'll be OK."

Patricia was holding on, too.

So was Wiande.

❖ ❖ ❖

Eric Armstead wasn't a certified agent, but he was partners with Brian Overstreet in E.O. Sports Management and, for all intents and purposes, he was Kevin's right-hand man. The agency had only 17 NFL players as clients, making it sort of a mom-and-pop store and enabling the agents to get more personally involved with the players they represented.

Kevin referred to Eric Armstead as "E," and the two became close friends. Their families went to dinner together, and Patricia

"I just kept thinking, 'I only hope he can walk again. I can't imagine Kevin going through life in a wheelchair.'"

would frequently make pecan candy for E's family.

Armstead had the NFL Sunday Ticket package in his Houston home, so he was able to watch Buffalo's season opener against Denver. As was his custom, he continually changed channels to keep an eye on several of his clients' games. When the Bills' game reached halftime, Armstead switched to another game, so he was caught off guard when Patricia phoned and frantically explained that Kevin had been injured on the second-half kickoff.

He clicked to the Bills game and saw Kevin down on the field, receiving medical attention.

"I told her everything would be OK," Armstead said, "and that it was a precautionary measure."

That's what he told her, but he had no way of knowing the extent of the injury. He immediately phoned John Guy, the Bills' director of pro personnel, to see if he had any information. Guy was in Cleveland, scouting the Bills' next opponent, the Pittsburgh Steelers, and had no information on Kevin.

"I'm sure he'll be all right," Guy told Armstead. "I'm sure they're just being safe."

"But he's not moving anything," Armstead said. "Call me if you hear anything."

After the game, Guy phoned Armstead and told him it was serious.

A few days later, Armstead boarded a plane to be by his friend's side. When he arrived at the hospital, even though doctors were much more optimistic than their original prognosis, Armstead was shocked by Kevin's appearance.

Kevin's eyes were closed, and tubes seemed to be all over his body.

Patricia leaned over his bed.

"Eric is here, Kevin."

"E" moved closer.

"Hang in there," Armstead said.

"If you can hear him, shake your head," Patricia said, softly.

Kevin, a tube in his mouth, mumbled something that was inaudible.

"He was still out of it," Armstead recalled.

Kevin was in a small room that was nearly filled to its capacity by the bed and machines that were pumping medicine into his system. There was barely room for a few visitors. The front part of the room had an opening that led to a circular area. When visitors stepped out of the room, they could see other patients in the beds next to Kevin's.

"He was next to an elderly woman who was badly burned," Armstead said. "It looked like a MASH unit."

Seeing Kevin look like he was at death's door alarmed Armstead. Kevin had the best physique of anyone Armstead had ever known; he was also always clean-shaven with neatly cropped hair. Now he had the start of a straggly beard, and medicine was being pumped into different parts of his ravaged body.

"I was shocked," Armstead said. "I just kept thinking, 'I only hope he can walk again. I can't imagine Kevin going through life in a wheelchair.'"

"E" left Buffalo after spending three days with Kevin. On his last day there, Kevin, mustering all the strength he could, barely got out his friend's name. "Hey, E," he said. And nothing else.

Kevin was still sedated. "E" was still wondering about Kevin's future. Three days in Buffalo had not eased his concerns. "I had doubts he would ever walk again," Armstead said.

Three days after his surgery, Kevin was still listed in critical condition, but Gibbons said he was pleased with rapidity of the recovery.

"The speed in which it's occurred is a great sign. Have we seen it before (in other patients)? Yes. In part, there are many things in his favor, including the fact he had deformity of his cord and not a transection and he never went into spinal shock," Gibbons said at a news conference. "But when we had talked about this before, during, and after the surgery, we discussed that this is a longshot for him to have a significant recovery of arms or legs, but certainly it's not impossible.

"For patients who have motor complete cervical injuries who have some preserved sensation, about 40 percent of them improve somewhat. Sometimes it's dramatic improvement that really means something. Sometimes it's the return of sensation.... Sometimes it's the return of useless motor movement."

She was amazed at the city's love for football... and for Kevin.

Gibbons said that sometimes a person "can push their knees together after surgery"—Kevin did that—"and three years later, all they can do is push their knees together. That's not useful motor. For many patients with cervical injuries, the ability to regain use of their hands, even if they don't regain the use of their legs, makes a huge difference in their independence."

For Kevin, for his family, it was a waiting game.

Kevin also had medical complications, including a collapsed lung and a paralyzed diaphragm, Gibbons said.

Kevin was still a very sick man.

❖ ❖ ❖

Wayetu Moore, Wiande's 22-year-old sister, heard about Kevin's injury while she was in Washington, D.C., where she was a journalism major at Howard University.

When her mom told her about the injury, Wayetu didn't realize its severity. "At first, I thought it was just something routine," she said. "I thought, 'I'll pray for him and he'll be OK.' We're a family of athletes and we're used to being injured, and I just thought it was a (typical) injury and everything would be all right."

But those thoughts soon changed when she learned the scope of the injury.

"I couldn't believe it. I felt so guilty for what I was thinking originally," she said.

Wayetu and her boyfriend, Donald Gray, a Howard senior, made the eight-hour drive to the Buffalo hospital.

She was amazed at the city's love for football...and for Kevin.

"There were cards and letters all over the room," she said, referring to the Everett family lounge that had been set up. "Boxes and boxes and boxes of cards. It really made me think that football is *the* American sport and that the city was so football-driven. I couldn't believe how supportive the people were."

Wayetu gave herself a little pep talk before walking into the room to visit with Kevin. She wanted to be strong for him, wanted to be positive.

"Initially, I was afraid to go in because I didn't know what to say," she said.

Then she remembered the time she and her boyfriend hung out with Kevin and Wiande in Manhattan. The four of them were returning from attending the Abyssinian Baptist Church, the oldest African-American church in New York City, and they were stuck in a traffic jam and began playing a word game called Wally's World. Kevin, known for his competitive streak, had been especially animated in playing the game.

So as Wayetu walked into Kevin's hospital room, she smiled, looked at him prone in the bed and said, "So, Kevin, want to play a game of Wally's World?" She had broken the ice.

Kevin still had a tube in his mouth, but he still managed to smirk. He shook his head as he said, "No," the word sounding muffled because the tube prevented him from speaking clearly. But his smile said he would one day be playing the game again and trying to beat the pants off everybody.

The smile alone was worth the eight-hour drive from D.C.

"That was enough for me—just knowing he was being responsive," Wayetu said.

❖❖❖

One week after his injury, Kevin was not only moving his toes but his entire leg.

"He continues to shock the doctors and those who underestimate him on a daily basis," Wiande said.

In her journal, Wiande was very spiritual:

"Get up, man. Please get up!" he said.

"God is wonderful and so good! His grace will and is working in this situation. His faithfulness to his children will ALWAYS remain the same...and it has.... The good Lord has his plans for Kevin and he knows the reasons and has the answers for everything."

Wiande was feeling exhausted; her entire body felt drained, but it felt good to sit next to Kevin and watch the Bills-Steelers game on the hospital-room TV. As a sign of support, Bills players wore T-shirts under their jerseys that had Everett's name and No. 85 printed on the back. Two days earlier, Patricia had addressed the Bills at their workout and given them an update on her son's condition. After she spoke, the Bills huddled and, in unison, let out a loud cheer for their fallen teammate.

"I cried and hugged as many of them as I could," Patricia said.

This was Buffalo's first game without Kevin. Wiande caressed his head and watched him closely "to make sure he was okay mentally." Earlier in the week, Kevin had become upset when a video of his collision with Hixon appeared on his TV. "Turn it off!" he snapped.

It was too painful to watch.

Wiande didn't want him agitated as he watched this game, but she couldn't control what happened: Steelers linebacker James Harrison was taken off the field on a stretcher with a neck injury on the final play of the first half. Kevin became emotional and began crying.

"Get up, man. Please get up!" he said. "I don't want this to happen to anybody else, man."

Wiande stroked his eyes and told him it would be okay.

Harrison was examined and then returned to the sideline midway through the third quarter and walked freely, but not before thoughts of Everett's situation raced through his mind. "They did, because he had just gotten hurt the previous week and we were playing against them, so yeah, thoughts of it went through my head," Harrison said. "But I didn't have the sensations that he described. I basically just had pain, so I wasn't really worried about paralysis or anything on that level."

After the game—the Bills dropped a 26–3 decision—Wiande went into the lobby and talked with Pastor Fred Raines, the Bills' unofficial chaplain, and Gretchen Geitter of the team's community-relations department before getting something to eat. While in the cafeteria, a nurse hurriedly walked toward Wiande and explained that Kevin wanted to see her.

Wiande had only been gone for a little while, but Kevin felt helpless without her by his side.

"Where were you? I thought you said five minutes, baby?" Kevin asked when she returned to the room.

"I'm sorry, baby," she said.

Wiande realized Kevin needed her and his mom to be with him around the clock.

"And that's exactly what we did," she said. "We were all he had in Buffalo at that moment."

Kevin drifted off to sleep. When he woke up, Wiande and Patricia were next to him.

"Wiande and Mrs. Patricia took turns being with him all day; they were there 24/7," said Wayetu, Wiande's sister. "Any time he wanted to talk or respond or do anything, he could feel their presence around him."

The day Wayetu and her boyfriend visited the hospital, Kevin kept coughing and spitting up. "He was real congested and Wiande placed a stack of Kleenex on his shoulder, and when he coughed, she took one off and was right there to wipe his mouth. My boyfriend just looked at me and it was like a look that said, 'I hope *you* would do this for me,'" Wayetu said with a soft smile. "She was just so attentive."

❖ ❖ ❖

Eight days after his surgery, Kevin's breathing had shown significant improvement. "The fact that he's a good athlete has helped," Gibbons said. "He has built-up chest muscles and muscles of the abdominal wall that have helped him breathe."

The medical news was getting better. Kevin was taken off the critical list, and many of his teammates were stopping by the hospital to make sure he remained upbeat. Roscoe Parrish was there, along with Josh Reed, Peerless Price, Brian Moorman, and J.P. Losman, among others.

"The love in the atmosphere was incredible," Wiande said. "I've never seen so many grown men cry before in my life."

Before going into the hospital room, Price promised that he wouldn't cry. "But he broke down, standing next to Kevin," Wiande said.

She was happy he did.

"It's good to cry," she said. "It's good to cry because crying mends your heart and allows you to express your true feelings about someone or a situation."

When the players left, Wiande and Kevin talked about their future.

"He told me that I'm his queen like always and that we will get married. I looked at him in his eyes and said, 'I know we will, baby, but you just focus on getting well right now. God will handle the rest,'" Wiande wrote in her journal. "He smiled and said, 'You're such a blessing. You know that I'm so happy! I love you.' I told him I'm happy I had him too."

Wiande fell asleep on Kevin's chest that night. When she woke up, she was in the room's recliner, not remembering how she got there.

❖ ❖ ❖

Eleven days after his surgery, Kevin continued to make strides, and it was announced that he would be transferred to a Houston hospital the next day to begin the next phase of his rehabilitation.

Dr. Barth Green, the colorful and outspoken Miami neurosurgeon who was a friend of the Buffalo Bills' president, had been receiving regular updates on Kevin's condition. After discussing the case with Cappuccino, the Bills' orthopedic surgeon, Green told reporters that "they're going to stand him up...soon. Now that doesn't mean he'll be walking normally, but standing up and holding his own weight. I think the future for him is very bright."

Doctors thought it would be best to move Kevin to Houston—where he would rehab in one of the nation's most respected facilities—because it was near his offseason home and his family and friends would help in his recovery.

"I love the Buffalo people and I'll hate to leave them," Patricia said. "But it'll be good that we can be closer to home for all our family to see him because they're worried about him. He wants to see his family, too."

Especially his sisters—Herchell, Kelli, and Davia.

Patricia Dugas said her son has had a positive outlook throughout the entire ordeal.

"Sometimes I walk around here saying, 'I can't believe he's smiling like that,'" she said. "That's what he gives me, peace. He keeps me strong."

❖❖❖

In her journal, Wiande noted that Kevin was making progress every day but that he continued to have leg spasms. She also noted that mail, addressed to Kevin, continued to overflow the front desk at Millard Fillmore Gates Hospital—and that the media continued to circle the premises.

"Everyone wants the story of Kevin Everett's progress," she wrote, "but in reality, it's sad to say, that's all they want—a story. Right now, Kevin needs to be resting and waiting patiently for a full recovery."

Back in Kevin's hospital room, Wiande was happy to see a man she called Kevin's "homeboy from Houston," Bills cornerback Jason Webster.

Webster had also been injured in the Bills' opener, and he wore a sling on his arm when he visited with Kevin. Webster, who had signed with Buffalo in the offseason, offered kind, reassuring words to his teammate.

He smiled at Kevin.

"I don't say this word enough, and sometimes we all don't use this word until something goes wrong, but I want to tell you that I love you," Webster said. "Anything you need, I'm here for you."

Wiande was deeply touched by Webster's show of affection for Kevin.

"I thought to myself, 'Wow. This is so true.' In life, we don't take time to say 'I love you' to those we love everyday. We fail to realize that life is not guaranteed."

❖ ❖ ❖

It was Thursday, September 20—11 days after the injury and the final full day they would spend in the Buffalo hospital.

Wiande arrived in Kevin's room at 10:00 AM; she relieved Patricia, who had to change and get ready for local interviews with the media.

A pleasant and gregarious woman, Patricia charmed the media with anecdotes about Kevin.

She said her son wasn't looking back, just ahead.

"He never asked 'Why?'" she said of the injury. "To tell you the truth, I think it's going to be all right. Kevin is a strong young man and he's not going to let this get him down. He's going to be fine. He's strong, you all. I'm telling you, he's strong. Kevin's going to get up walking and take care of his business, like he always does."

It wasn't going to be that simple. There was still a lot of work to be done before Kevin could even *think* about walking. He was still confined to a bed and unable to sit up for any significant amount of time.

Kevin was also starting to get frustrated and angry. During his final full day at the Buffalo hospital, those outside the room could hear Kevin screaming at Wiande and demanding to see his mother.

"I had never seen him act that way before," Wiande said, "but I could only imagine what he was going through."

She calmly stepped out of the room to get Mrs. Patricia.

Kevin later apologized, and things calmed down. Patricia slept in one of the hospital rooms, and Wiande slept on the recliner in Kevin's room. The next morning, a private plane would take them on an early flight to Houston's Hobby Airport.

Wiande woke up at 5:00 AM, showered, and then met with Dr. Cappuccino and other medical staff members who were bagging Kevin's personal belongings and placing them by the door. The paramedics came in with a stretcher, and Wiande and Patricia signed release forms to fly on the private plane. When they got outside, security guards were everywhere. Wiande and Patricia said their goodbyes to some of the Millard Fillmore Gates medical team and to Paul Lancaster, the Bills' director of player programs, and Gretchen Geitter, the team's executive director of community relations.

Tears rolled down Wiande's cheeks as she hugged Geitter.

Some were tears of joy, "but in the back of my mind, some were tears for the journey ahead," Wiande said, "and for the strength that I needed to show for Kevin."

"

As I stared at the banner, I knew that it would only be a matter of time before my love would be up and walking again. I knew that God's love and his grace will continue to be with Kevin and with us during this time.

—Wiande's journal entry, September 21, 2007

"

As they placed Kevin in an ambulance, Wiande looked to the right and saw a huge banner with an image of Kevin in his Buffalo Bills uniform, holding a football in his hand. "Warrior... Keep Fighting!" the banner said.

The group arrived at the Buffalo airport at around 6:40 AM and loaded their belongings on the private plane. Before they left, one of the paramedics—a man who had been beside Kevin after his accident—handed Wiande a box that contained a hospital robe his wife had made for the football-player-turned-patient. Kevin, Wiande, and Patricia said their final good-byes, boarded the plane, and headed for Houston.

The Buffalo medical personnel, the Bills, and the fans had

been incredible, but Wiande was happy Kevin was going to be near his roots for the next phase of his recovery.

"We're excited to be going back home," she said.

The flight to Houston was smooth, and Kevin and his group arrived at Memorial Hermann|TIRR (The Institute for Rehabilitation and Research) just before 10:00 AM. When they got out of the limo that had transported them to the hospital, they were greeted by cameras. Lots and lots of cameras. The hospital staff tried to cover Kevin to give him his privacy, but later in the week, a photo was on the front page of the *Houston Chronicle*.

"The media just won't rest, huh?" said Wiande's journal entry.

The first day was chaotic for everyone. Doctors, nurses, therapists, more doctors, and respiratory therapists were in and out of Kevin's hospital room all day.

There was an awkward moment when Kevin, naked, was examined thoroughly by some nurses while Wiande was in the room.

"As I stood next to him, he looked at me ashamed because here I was, his girl, looking at him unrobed with other women in the room," Wiande wrote in her journal. "It was so embarrassing for him. I just had to tough it up and accept the fact that, right now, my man is in this situation where women have to see him, but I know that he looks in my face for strength, and I have to continue to remain strong for him. And that's exactly what I did."

Wiande went home for a while, showered, changed, and then returned to the hospital. Mrs. Patricia and her three daughters were still there. Two of Kevin's sisters, Herchell and Kelli, and Wiande spent the night with Kevin.

"We did different shifts because we only had a sofa bed and a recliner chair, so we had to alternate sleeping arrangements," Wiande said. "We survived. We had to."

CHAPTER 6

HOUSTON, WE HAVE
A PROBLEM

"He didn't want the lights on. He didn't want people to see him
and he stayed like that for three whole weeks.
I think he was anxious about people seeing a lack of
movement because he was used to being
a big, powerful guy. He didn't want people to see him
like that. Then he saw other people
in the gym and saw how fortunate he was."

He couldn't feed himself, couldn't stand, couldn't sit, couldn't bathe, couldn't groom himself. He was confined to a bed, dependent on everybody else around him. It's no wonder that Kevin Everett, back in his home state, was somewhat withdrawn during his early days at Memorial Hermann | TIRR, located in the world-renowned Texas Medical Center in Houston.

Worth Whiteside, a social worker at TIRR, met with Kevin, Wiande, and Kevin's mom, Patricia, during their hectic first day at the rehabilitation center. Whiteside gave the trio a sense of what was going to happen early in his stay. He told them he was available to talk about any of their concerns and explained that this was going to be a long, ever-evolving process.

The social worker was part of a group that became known as Team Kevin. The group included Dr. Teodoro "Ted" Castillo, Kevin's attending physician; Darryn Atkinson, physical therapist; Rafferty Laredo, occupational therapist; Dawn Brown, recreational therapist; Barbara Jackson, case manager; and assorted nurses.

Kevin's second day at TIRR was also hectic. Medical personnel made constant checkups, and nurses came into his room every two hours to turn him, attempting to prevent bed sores. For the most part, Kevin was upbeat, "but every now and then he has emotional fits and gets down," Wiande said, "but who wouldn't in his situation? It's only natural for him to feel this way, and I'm going to be here to support him and be strong for him no matter what because he needs me to be strong."

"He didn't like me. He thought I was going to be like a drill sergeant."

In his third day at TIRR, Kevin was bothered by severe pain in his neck and discomfort from the catheter. He was taking medication for the pain, and he told doctors he still had no feeling in his arms.

Kevin arrived at the Houston hospital on a Friday. Four days later, the first of Kevin's "team rounds" was held. Members of Team Kevin would meet every Tuesday with Kevin and Wiande to discuss the progress that was being made. Or the lack of it.

In the initial meeting on September 25, Kevin was quiet and unexpressive.

> **"** *The most important thing about Kevin in this situation is that he focuses on getting better and nothing else. He doesn't need to worry about anything because when he worries, it doesn't help the situation. It only makes it worse.*
>
> —Wiande's journal entry,
> September 22, 2007 **"**

"He was still dealing with a whole bunch of stuff and getting used to being in the hospital," said Whiteside, the social worker. "He didn't have a lot to say. He was in a room with folks he had only known for a few days and he was distant."

Laredo, the occupational therapist, also made note of Kevin's withdrawn state. It was typical, he thought, for someone who was a professional athlete and now didn't know if he would be able to do anything on his own. Ever. It was Laredo's mission to help Kevin regain independence to do simple life tasks—brushing his teeth, lifting a fork or spoon to his mouth, washing his face, wiping himself after a bowel movement. The list was endless.

Atkinson, a physical therapist with a shaved head and a muscular physique, later learned that Kevin wasn't particularly fond of him in their first few meetings.

"He didn't like me," Atkinson said. "He thought I was going to be like a drill sergeant."

Atkinson's job was to help Kevin regain mobility and do things most people take for granted. The first goal was to get Kevin to move around in bed and be able to get in and out of it. Eventually, Atkinson hoped to help Kevin be able to stand, sit in a chair, and to use a wheelchair. A long-range goal was to get Kevin to stand and then walk.

Atkinson pushed Kevin, who gradually learned to trust the therapist's skills.

When Kevin arrived at TIRR, which has been named one of "America's Best Hospitals" by *U.S. News & World Report* for 18 consecutive years, he needed assistance to move in bed.

"His trunk was the most affected, so (lying) down was very difficult," Atkinson said.

In Kevin's first few days at TIRR, he was in a tilted wheelchair.

"He wasn't in a wheelchair yet when he got here, so what we do is get him in a reclining chair, because low blood pressure is usually the biggest issue, and the tone of the muscles is greatly reduced, and so they have problems with low blood pressure when they go from sitting to standing," Atkinson said.

When Kevin would sit all the way up, "all the blood would kind of go in his legs," Atkinson said, "and he'd get real dizzy." Trying to stabilize Kevin's blood pressure was one of the medical team's many goals.

Team Kevin had a lot of obstacles, including the patient's 6'4" frame, which made it more difficult to go from a sitting to a standing position.

During his first week at TIRR, Kevin was able to sit in a tilted wheelchair. It would take another 10 days before he could sit up straight in the wheelchair and not have his blood pressure affected.

The blood-pressure problem is common among spinal-cord patients. "What happens basically is that the input from the brain is cut off from your legs, so what happens is the tone in your legs a lot of time goes down a lot," Atkinson said. "The tone of your muscles is what helps the blood return to your heart; it keeps your blood pressure up, so when you lose that, and once the blood goes to your feet, it's a lot harder to get it up. It kind of tends to stay there."

During his early days at TIRR, Kevin worked with Atkinson on simple exercises, such as sitting on a bed—and finding out how long he could do it without having someone assist him. Once that was accomplished, Atkinson worked on having Kevin get into a better sitting posture, where he was sitting up tall.

Getting Kevin to stand was also part of the plan.

"We just worked on functional activities," Atkinson said. "They were the goals we had."

❖ ❖ ❖

For Kevin, there was a "feeling out" period between himself and the medical staff at The Institute for Rehabilitation and Research—at least that's how the TIRR staff members perceived it.

One week into his stay at TIRR, Laredo, the occupational therapist, was still attempting to form a bond with Kevin, still attempting to earn his trust.

During parts of his first two weeks in the Houston hospital, Everett seemed overwhelmed by Team Kevin.

"I think at that point, he was wondering, 'Who are these people that I'm entrusting to help me through this recovery process?'" Laredo said. "And to a certain degree, he was sort of assessing us and was concerned, as anyone should be, whether or not we were the right team for him."

In an attempt to see what made Kevin click and to find out about his pre-injury personality, Laredo asked the football player a few questions.

"How would your friends or your teammates describe you?" he wondered.

"They would say I have a good personality and I'm funny," Kevin replied, "and that I like to play practical jokes and like to have a good time."

Kevin's response surprised Laredo.

"It was interesting," Laredo said, "because at that time, that wasn't the Kevin that I saw and knew."

In time, the medical team hoped, the kidding with therapists and the practical jokes would become a daily part of Kevin's existence at TIRR.

If Laredo began observing the real Kevin, he knew things would be moving on the right path.

If.

"I knew that when I started to see that personality emerge," Laredo said, "that things were all right for him in his eyes."

Atkinson, the physical therapist, remembered Kevin being in a somber mood during his first few weeks at TIRR. "When he first got here, it was always dark in his room. All the lights were off, the curtains (closed)…and the shades were pulled down," Atkinson said.

He would ask Kevin if he wanted him to bring light into the room. Kevin declined.

"He didn't want the lights on," Atkinson said. "He didn't want people to see him and he stayed like that for three whole weeks. I think he was anxious about people seeing a lack of movement because he was used to being a big, powerful guy. He didn't want people to see him like that. Then he saw other people in the gym and saw how fortunate he was."

Kevin's fascination with darkness was understandable for someone in his predicament. It was only natural, Atkinson said, to feel anxious and wonder "whether or not it was going to happen again."

That, combined with the assessment period with his medical team, contributed to Kevin's guarded personality for a few weeks.

In Laredo's case, he wondered if there wasn't another factor involved: his small stature. "I'm not a big guy. I have a pretty small frame," said the 5'9", 145-pound occupational therapist. "And I think he was really anxious. It was like, 'Who is this little kid that's treating me?' Kevin is a stout guy, so I think there was a part of him that thought, 'Who's this little person that's going to essentially make me stronger?'"

"I knew that when I started to see that personality emerge," Laredo said, "that things were all right for him in his eyes."

It would take time, Laredo thought, before the medical team and Kevin were all on the same page.

❖ ❖ ❖

Dawn Brown, a recreational therapist with a hard-driving style that contradicted her 4'10" frame, chatted with Kevin and made a complete evaluation during his first day at the Houston rehabilitation hospital.

It was Brown's goal to help improve Kevin's functional ability and to provide education and training regarding recreational activities—and to promote social interaction and healthy living through those activities.

Brown chatted with Kevin and learned that he liked to shoot pool, do things with Wiande, and play table games. Football was not mentioned.

He was very serious and had a "flat" demeanor, Brown thought.

"Kevin was nice and answered all my questions," Brown said, "but there was definitely sadness in his face and sadness in his tone."

The room was dark, and Kevin had electric fans blowing on him and the air-conditioner was turned on. As Brown started to leave the room, she asked Kevin if he needed anything. She sensed that Kevin wanted her to stay and hang out for a while,

that he needed company. They talked for a while. Brown told
Kevin about her two teenage children. Kevin talked about Wiande
and his family. Kevin was still a bit guarded, but a bond was
starting to build.

Brown met Wiande the next day and, for the longest time, she
had difficulty remembering how to pronounce her name.

"WAY-ahn-DEE," she would say.

Or "WEE-ahn-DAY."

"WEE-Ahn-DEE," she was politely corrected.

In the coming weeks, Wiande twice handed Brown a piece
of paper with the correct pronunciation printed on it. Brown's
name-butchering became a running joke between herself, Kevin,
and Wiande.

From the moment she first observed Kevin and Wiande, Brown
marveled at their connection. She could see how much they loved
each other, how much they respected and supported one another.

*"I think just being outside
was a bigger benefit
than any of the physical
things we did."*

"They are definitely best friends,"
Brown said. "Wiande is *always* in
his corner, and Kevin is so proud of
her and her accomplishments. They
watch each other and smile and
laugh together a lot."

During Kevin's first few weeks
at TIRR, Brown made it a point not
to talk about football unless Kevin
mentioned it. It never became a part of their conversation.

The first time Brown saw Kevin for therapy, she told him she
wanted to take him outside. A look of concern covered Kevin's
face. Brown assured him that she would take him to a place
where no photos could be taken of him by the media. He was
nervous about it, but at the same time, seemed to want to get out
into the sun.

"I really felt he needed to get out of his dark, sheltered room," Brown said, "and it was a gorgeous day."

She took him to the courtyard, a pretty area filled with flowers and oak trees near a patient-used greenhouse in the back of the hospital. Brown brought out a deck of cards. They began working on moving Kevin's arms to push the cards a few inches on the table.

Kevin, sitting in his wheelchair, seemed pleased to be out of his hospital room.

"I think just being outside was a bigger benefit than any of the physical things we did," Brown said. "Getting your head right and getting as comfortable as you can in any situation benefits all parties involved. From that point on, if the weather was good, we were outside."

Brown used slings to support Kevin's arms and they worked on movement…and control of the movement. Even though Kevin was a strong man, small movements would fatigue him quickly. After a few sessions, the two had a flourishing rapport. They would kid about each others' strengths and weaknesses. Brown would also give Kevin a hard time about keeping his hospital room dark.

Even sitting in a wheelchair, Kevin was taller than the blonde-haired Brown as she stood. Size didn't matter. She challenged Kevin to his limits with her drills. Kevin responded.

"He was not afraid to try anything new," Brown said, "and I wasn't afraid to push him."

Wiande was always nearby, jotting down notes in her ever-present journal. In the evening, Wiande and Kevin would go outside and spend time in the courtyard behind the hospital.

Sitting in the garden area was therapeutic to Kevin and Wiande.

"I think it was their way to get away from everything and just be them," Brown said. "I'm sure it must be hard to have to be nice to everyone and also constantly have to watch your back for people or the press trying to get a picture or a look. A slip up by getting aggravated or angry—which with the average patient is very normal—to the wrong person that is willing to go to the press, and Kevin's reputation could be ruined."

Angriness, however, was rarely a part of Kevin's makeup. Or Wiande's. They had each other, and they had hope. There was no need for anger.

❖❖❖

During his early days at TIRR, Kevin Everett, who months earlier was a world-class athlete, was unable to lift a spoon to his mouth.

It was too heavy.

When Everett arrived at TIRR, he weighed about 223 pounds—32 pounds lighter than his playing weight of 255. He was in a weakened state and required assistance to do even menial tasks.

Including trying to lift a spoon and feed himself.

To compensate, Kevin used a device called a universal cuff, which is essentially like a little bucket that you attach to your hand and the utensils slide into it.

Laredo was trying to discover what kind of potential Kevin had with his arms and legs; he worked with Kevin on several exercises. Some were designed to get Kevin's shoulders stable enough so they could move. Another tried to get his arms to touch his mouth so he could take a wash cloth to his face. Another attempted to make his grip strong enough to hold a utensil and be able to feed himself.

The drills bore little resemblance to the grinding summer workouts with the Bills during training camp at St. John Fisher College in Rochester, New York, but these exercises were much more important. They would help Kevin regain his independence.

To help speed the muscles' return, Laredo had Kevin do repetitive drills in which he gripped and squeezed a rubber ball. He also had Kevin open and close his hands, slowly and then quickly.

Kevin began making rapid progress. Soon, he was able to grip a normal utensil and didn't need to use a special one that made it easier to hold.

"Some of the initial things we did were just a hand-to-mouth pattern or the ability to touch his face or be able to reach the top of his head," Laredo said. "In terms of intervention, he had a lot of weakness in his shoulders, and his arms were really heavy just because they're big and he didn't have the joint support in order to hold them up without pain."

Kevin had a high pain tolerance, however, and rarely complained.

"Essentially, it was as if his arms were kind of pulled out of their sockets," Laredo said. "That's probably the easiest way to describe it, and that made it really challenging to do things like standing and walking because if he were to stand up or walk, the weight of his arms created so much pain in his shoulders and in the neck. That's why we started with a walker with a platform to support his arms."

❖ ❖ ❖

Virgil Calhoun, a jovial sort with a big belly and a bigger smile, seemed unlikely to be the person that Kevin would eventually lean on as he tried to make his recovery.

At 56, Virgil was more than twice Kevin's age, and he wasn't a big football fan. But Virgil, a chemical technician who loved talking about food (especially catfish, dirty rice, and anything with barbecue sauce on it), and Kevin found common ground: Both had been paralyzed, and both were now at TIRR trying to become independent again.

In the summer of 2007, while in another hospital, Virgil had received an epidural in an attempt to ease his excruciating neck pain.

The operation was a disaster.

"When I came out of the anesthesia, I couldn't move my left side," he said.

He eventually was transferred to TIRR on September 13, eight days before Kevin arrived there.

Before Kevin's arrival at the Houston hospital, patients had been advised to keep their distance from the NFL player and give him his privacy. They respected it.

"It became a challenge. I challenged him and he challenged me. It's like you do on a basketball court, trying to stick it to each other."

Kevin was flat on his back during his early days at TIRR. Within his first week at the facility, he was in the hospital's gym, and it wasn't unusual to see him lying on one of the gym's mats and working with a therapist to regain movement.

Virgil, then using a walker to get around, would see Kevin as he went through his own routine in the gym. He would nod or smile, but he kept his distance. He understood that Kevin needed his privacy.

Or at least that's what he thought. It turned out that Kevin needed Virgil more than his solitude. Lying on the mat, Kevin spotted the 6'3", 238-pound Virgil moving past him on his walker.

"Hey, big man," Kevin said.

"Hey, what's happening?" Virgil replied. He gave Kevin a "thumbs-up" sign and continued on his way.

A couple of days later, Kevin, with security guards around him to keep autograph-seekers away, started a conversation with

Virgil. They've been talking ever since.

Virgil would go on the treadmill and make sure he told Kevin that he went three miles.

Eventually, Kevin would try to match it.

"He'd say, 'Man, you're doing good. I want to get where you're at.' I'd say, 'Come on, then. You have to catch up,'" Virgil said. "He said, 'I will. I will.'"

They began comparing times, comparing the amount of weight they could lift, comparing how many reps they could do.

"We pushed each other," Kevin said.

"It became a challenge," Virgil said. "I challenged him and he challenged me. It's like you do on a basketball court, trying to stick it to each other."

Their rapport became so strong that Virgil stayed in the gym even after his session was over, just so he could be with Kevin.

"I said to myself, 'I have to stick around and just mess with him a little bit and encourage him,'" Virgil said.

"They're so good for each other," Wiande said. "Kevin is soooo competitive; he plays to win."

Without knowing it, Virgil pushed him. And vice versa.

Virgil needed the pushing "more than Kevin," said Lyn Calhoun, Virgil's wife. "I really was glad the relationship developed because I tried to push Virgil (in his rehab) at home, but with Kevin, and two men talking trash, it made him be more motivated."

"Kevin would see Mr. Virgil doing something and he'd say, 'You'd better watch out. I'm coming to get you. I'm going to be on the courts in a couple of weeks and I'm going to get you,'" Wiande said after sharing a meal with Kevin, Virgil, and Lyn at a local restaurant. "And that just motivated Mr. Virgil even more. Kevin would be on the treadmill and he'd come up to Kevin and talk more noise and say, 'Well, I did 2.5 miles today. How many are you going to do?' It was just trash talking back and forth, but it was out of love, you know."

❖ ❖ ❖

To find other ways of motivation, all Kevin and Virgil had to do was look around the rectangle-shaped gym at TIRR. The gym has numerous mats, weight machines, a basketball backboard, a treadmill, a stationary bike, and other assorted exercise equipment. Two framed basketball jerseys from the TIRR Hotwheels—the hospital's wheelchair team of 10- to 18-year-old players—hang proudly on one of the walls.

Above the gym, there are 48 small windows at the top of two walls, and they allow light to splash into the room.

But the real sunshine is provided by the hard-working patients.

Some work on arm weights while sitting in wheelchairs. Some are minus a limb, but it doesn't deter their determination. All have a purpose—getting on with their lives and being able to do the "little things" again—with an almost unimaginable dedication.

"They inspire me," Everett said.

In one corner of the room, a 50ish-looking man walks on a treadmill with a harness around his shoulders for support. He is regaining leg motion, and sweat drips from his brow as he looks straight ahead, never wavering, never complaining to the therapist who assists him and pushes him.

"How can you look around here and not feel inspired?" Everett asked, rhetorically.

Everett said, "Everybody here is an inspiration to me," but he singled out one patient in particular, a man named Nate. "He came here about the same time I did and he had a brain injury and couldn't talk and didn't know anything," Kevin said. "Just seeing him every day and seeing how much he's progressed is amazing. I mean, each day you see it, and now he's recognizing me and he knows me."

Kevin shook his head.

"It's not only him. It's everybody here," he said. "From not knowing what's going on to (making improvement) and being released and going home in a matter of months."

Most of the patients are at TIRR because of brain or spinal-cord injuries, strokes, amputations, or progressive neurological disorders, such as multiple sclerosis. Some have been in car accidents, some have suffered gang-related trauma, some have endured sports injuries, and some have been involved in various other mishaps.

"At TIRR, you have to be motivated. And if you think you've got it bad, you look at other people and you see they're worse off than you are, but they get around," Virgil said. "They have a positive attitude and that's what you have to keep around here. Everything is a challenge to do better, to do better, to do better. Since I've been on the treadmill, sometimes I get an audience staring at me and they're amazed at how far I've come. I came here flat on my back and couldn't move…and look at me now…. They got me moving around, using the walker."

When Virgil and Kevin talk, there is little conversation about stocks (Virgil's passion) or football. Instead, they center around Kevin's mom's gumbo and Lyn's homemade cooking that has satiated Kevin's sweet tooth (especially her lemon cheesecake). They even get around to talking about bodily functions and how they are struggling to regulate their slow-moving bowels since their injuries.

But most of the conversation is about their quest to keep moving ahead, to keep on reaching another little milestone that will make them more independent.

They are shining examples of resiliency, but there are dozens of other such examples in the same room. All of them toil in a gym that has TIRR's unofficial mascot—Prometheus breaking from shackles—painted on one of the walls. In Greek mythology, Prometheus was a titan who became a hero to mankind when he stole fire from the gods and gave it to them. According to one myth, Prometheus was tortured by Zeus for stealing fire from heaven and giving it to mankind. Prometheus, the myth goes, was rescued by Hercules.

Prometheus and Hercules sound like pretty good teammates. Like Kevin and Virgil.

❖ ❖ ❖

While at TIRR, some patients have told Kevin they use him as a role model.

"I tell them they're my inspiration, right back," Kevin said. "Just like you're feeding off me, I'm feeding right back off you. I give them the sense that somebody looks up to them, also. Not only because of who I am. It just makes me feel good, though, to actually be able to see the value of life and how to cherish it. I mean, we take things for granted until something happens."

"He gave me hope. He made me work harder. He was my miracle for Christmas."

What happened to Amanda Brugmann in the winter of 2006 was an accident that left her as a paraplegic. Sitting in a wheelchair, paralyzed from the chest down, she visited TIRR to have an outpatient test administered in late December.

By chance, she rolled right past Everett, who was working with a physical therapist in the hospital's gym.

Brugmann, 32, knew all about Everett, whose odds-defying recovery had been the cover story in *Sports Illustrated* the previous week. She had also followed his progress on the Buffalo Bills' website and in a Port Arthur newspaper.

"I just wanted to tell you that you motivate me," Brugmann

said in her chance meeting with Kevin.

"Thank you. How are you doing?" Kevin asked.

In their brief conversation, Brugmann didn't get into the specifics about her injury. Later, she said she was drunk and high on cocaine when she tried to cross a Texas street and was hit by a car on February 27, 2006. There was no need to discuss that with Kevin.

"I'm doing well," she said.

Brugmann's wide smile and teary eyes gave the impression that the brief encounter would have a lasting effect.

"When I read about his injury, I prayed for him all the time," she said after Kevin began doing a workout with one of his therapists. "And he inspired me to work hard."

A teacher's aide, Brugmann said her accident actually "saved my life" because she said she was an addict at the time of her injury. She has been clean and sober for two years, she said.

After returning to her home in Nederland, Texas, following her unexpected meeting with Kevin, Brugmann felt inspired and began using her specially designed exercise equipment more frequently. "He gave me hope," she said. "He made me work harder. He was my miracle for Christmas."

TIRR, a 116-bed nonprofit hospital that was founded in 1959, continues to help her learn how to do things independently, such as cooking, she said.

"This place," she said, "has changed my life."

Kevin Everett could relate.

❖ ❖ ❖

By the end of September, Kevin needed just moderate assistance to have bed mobility, and he began working with Darryn Atkinson, his physical therapist, in an attempt to go from a sitting to a standing position.

For Kevin, who was taking medication to alleviate his neck

pain—and wearing a neck brace to provide stability—it was a struggle. Atkinson did maybe three-quarters of the work as he got Kevin into a standing position. He was only able to stand for a minute or two, mainly because the blood-pressure issues would make him dizzy. He also wasn't strong enough to stand for long, but his strength began to increase. Some of the strength returned naturally as he moved further away from the injury. Some of it returned because of the exercises he was doing.

Kevin was getting out of bed more easily and, as his blood pressure became regulated, there was hope that the one-time star athlete, the man who displayed an off-the-charts 42-inch vertical leap in college, would attempt to walk in a week or two.

CHAPTER 7
A HOSPITAL WEDDING PROPOSAL

"I truly feel like it did make our relationship stronger
and it was just like God saying,
'You don't need to be anywhere else,
anyplace else, but with him.'"

There may be more romantic places to propose than in a hospital rehab center. Then again, when you understand how Kevin and Wiande's relationship went to another level after the catastrophic injury, perhaps it was the *perfect* setting.

"To be honest, we were having some problems before this happened," Kevin said. "This brought us closer together. To have her by my side, I feel blessed."

Wiande was by Kevin's side almost every second of every day. She carried around spiral notebooks and kept track of Kevin's medical records and progress, his peaks and his valleys. She wrote down what he ate for breakfast, lunch, and dinner, and all the drills that the therapists had him perform. She wrote down his weight fluctuations, his mood, his accomplishments in the gym.

In short, she wrote down everything that pertained to Kevin—even his urine output—and his rehabilitation.

The hospital workers noticed.

"They'd see me and they'd say, 'Here comes the investigator, about to ask 100 questions!'" she said.

She smiled.

"I had to make sure they were doing things right," she explained.

On September 26, Wiande, Patricia, Herchel (Kevin's stepdad), and the three girls visited with Kevin, who was feeling well and getting ready for what was supposed to be an intense therapy session the next day.

When Patricia and her group left, Kevin and Wiande talked for a while about their future together. As Wiande caressed his hair, Kevin looked into her dark brown eyes.

"I love you, baby.... I'm ready, baby. Will you marry me?"

Wiande, standing near Kevin's bed, was stunned.

"I had to talk to myself and ask, 'Is he *really* proposing to me?'" she said.

By the look in Kevin's eyes, Wiande knew he was being sincere, knew this was a moment she had always imagined—though she didn't figure it would happen from a hospital bed.

"Yes!" she said.

In her journal that night, Wiande wrote that after Kevin proposed, "I didn't even cry because I knew that this day would come in God's time. Though I wanted it on my time, God does things when he wants to.... This night was the best night of my life."

❖ ❖ ❖

Wiande and Kevin, each of whom became elite athletes, have vastly different backgrounds. Kevin grew up in a one-parent family and—aside from his days at the University of Miami and with the Buffalo Bills—has lived in Texas his entire life. Wiande, the daughter of an engineer (her dad) and Catholic school teacher (her mom), survived a civil war in Liberia, where she lived until she was seven. She has also lived in New York City; Stratford, Connecticut; Memphis, Tennessee; and Spring, Texas.

The fact they found each other brings joy to those around them, especially Mamawa Moore, Wiande's mom.

"Kevin and Wiande have a beautiful relationship based on mutual faith in God, love and respect for each other and their family members," she said, adding that the couple has "a selfless love that makes each put the other's needs and well being first. Kevin will do anything for Wiande, and Wiande will do anything for Kevin. That's the agape love that caused Wiande to get on the plane the day after Kevin's injury, leaving her teaching and coaching job at Spring High School to be by his side. That's the love that makes you know they are going to succeed, no matter what obstacles they face in life."

The morning after Kevin proposed, Wiande washed and dressed him to get ready for his physical therapy. Later that day,

Mamawa visited with Kevin at the Buffalo hospital.

"Did you tell her?" Kevin excitedly asked Wiande, who was also standing by his bed.

"Tell me what?" Mamawa replied.

Wiande happily supplied the details.

"Mom, Kevin proposed to me last night!" she said.

Mamawa was thrilled with the news.

"I was very happy because I know that they had gotten to that level in their relationship," she said. "They love each other and I believe they are ready for marriage. Of course, being my first daughter and the oldest in the family, there was a feeling of nostalgia, but I was very happy for both Kevin and Wiande. I have gained a son, and he is the most respectful, loving, and selfless young man. I feel blessed to have him as my future son-in-law, and I am happy that Wiande is marrying the man she loves."

The day after the proposal had been a joyous one for Kevin and Wiande; they were sharing their plans with Wiande's mom when Patricia entered the room.

Patricia seemed upset.

"Can I talk to my son alone, please?" she said.

Wiande and her mom stepped out of the room. When they returned a short time later, Patricia began crying.

"She was basically my mom and my dad, just raising me the best way she could. She tried hard and she did a good job with it. Just look at me now."

Wiande gave her a hug "because I know she does not want to let go of her son.... She was always ready for us to get married, but now I know that every mother deep down inside has a problem with letting go."

Wiande understood Mrs. Patricia's feelings. Patricia had been a single parent to Kevin for most of his younger years, and their bond was even stronger than most mothers and sons. One day, Wiande thought, she hoped to have a son and hoped to experience the same closeness that Mrs. Patricia and Kevin share.

"She's a very special lady and she means everything to me," Kevin said. "She was basically my mom *and* my dad, just raising me the best way she could. She tried hard and she did a good job with it. Just look at me now. I mean, every spanking I got, I deserved it. Every fussing she ever gave me, I deserved it.

"She means everything to me."

Three days after he proposed, Kevin asked his longtime friend Tony Tompkins to pick him up at the hospital. Tony drove him to a jewelry store at the mall, where Kevin picked out a three-piece ring set. Wiande was ecstatic with his selection.

"He wants to do things on his own and wants to make sure it's very special," Wiande said. "He puts a lot of thought into everything he does."

At the hospital later that day, Kevin had many visitors. Herchell, Kelli, and Davia conversed with their big brother. Mrs. Patricia and her husband were also there, along with Eric Armstead, Kevin's representative. Some were in the room and some stood in the adjacent hallway.

Herchell was massaging Kevin's shoulders, and the entire room became quiet as Wiande and her mom, Mamawa, entered. Wiande pulled out the ring boxes.

"I looked at my mama and she smiled at me," Wiande said. "Her smile reassured me that everything will be OK."

The silence in the room was unbearable.

Finally, Kevin declared, "Baby, hold the rings up!"

The couple received congratulations, and a short time later, Wiande phoned her sister, Wayetu, and excitedly asked her to be the maid of honor for their 2009 wedding. Wayetu was elated.

"We've dreamed of being each other's maid of honor for a long time," Wayetu said, "and now that's it's actually here, it seems a little unbelievable. We've always been the Moore sisters. We've always done stuff together and even as we get older we do things together."

Wayetu described Wiande and Kevin's relationship as "very traditional and spiritual. They are both so humble. Kevin makes Wiande a priority in his life, and he tries his best to make Wiande happy. Wiande reciprocates with her loyalty and full companionship. It's like they've both blocked out their peripheral views, where the thought of being with—or even look at—others is out of the question, because what they've found is exactly what they've both always wanted."

Dawn Brown, the recreational therapist at TIRR, was excited to hear about Kevin's proposal. The couple, she thought, seem so natural together.

"Wiande and Kevin are such a mature, down-to-earth couple for being as young as they are," she said. Kevin is 25. Wiande is 24. "They complement each other and just have *it*. They know where they are and also where they came from. They appreciate what they have and I think they are okay with what they don't have, no matter what that may be. Many times in the rehab process, we as therapists see relationships and marriages crumble for various reasons.

"Wiande and Kevin have stood solid!"

The couple is planning a wedding for the fall of 2009, and Kevin's 23-year-old cousin, Chris Adams, will be his best man. Chris and Kevin grew up together in Port Arthur, Texas, and shared the same bedroom for a while at their Grandpa's house. Kevin will never forget his roots, never forget the people who have been important in his life.

The feeling is mutual.

"He's always been right by my side," Chris said. "I always looked up to him; he showed me right from wrong. You don't forget that."

Kevin and Wiande both say that his life-threatening injury made their relationship stronger.

"I think it did draw us closer because it was like a long-term relationship," Wiande said of the time they have spent together during the rehab.

In a way, they had lived separate lives. Wiande was a 10th-grade English teacher and track coach at the Spring High, the Texas school in which she was an academic and athletic standout. Kevin was traveling around the country with the Buffalo Bills.

They spent time together in the offseason.

"When he was first drafted by Buffalo, I was still in school in Miami and running track," Wiande said. "And, like the average NFL player, you're going to have questions like, 'Is he faithful? Is he cheating?' I got that—people were just coming in with questions, but the relationship was based on trust and communication—and I feel like that is what brought us closer together."

She paused.

> "
>
> *Kevin practiced sitting up in bed. He did this for about five minutes. He practiced sitting up (with the therapist's hands behind him), then she removed her hands and he was sitting by himself. I was so proud of him. Then, he stood up. He looked so different, but to me, he was still my Kevin. The most handsome man in the world. When he stood up, tears sat in my eyes. I was so happy! I looked at Herchell and she smiled at me, and I smiled at her. Kelli smiled at me and I winked at her. We were all so happy because today he made one step closer to what the doctors were saying he couldn't do. God is truly amazing!*
>
> —Wiande' journal entry,
> September 29, 2007
>
> "

"And then when this accident happened, it finally made me realize that this is the person who I'm supposed to be with. So I truly feel like it did make our relationship stronger and it was just like God saying, 'You don't need to be anywhere else, anyplace else, but with him.'"

When Kevin was on the road with the Bills, Wiande kept in touch with him primarily by phone and text-messaging. And since Kevin isn't a big talker on the phone, they communicated mostly in text messages.

After graduating from Miami, Wiande returned to Texas to teach. The relationship was still a long-distance one.

"It was hard. I'm not going to say it was easy, but every relationship is hard," Wiande said. "And it's when trying times come that you finally realize if this is what you want to do or be in."

❖❖❖

Before settling in Texas, Wiande's family had made a remarkable journey. Mamawa Moore, Wiande's mom, left her family in Liberia to pursue her master's degree in education at Columbia University on a prestigious Fulbright scholarship. The thinking was for her to return to Liberia after she finished school, "but that was not God's plan for our life," Mamawa said.

They didn't have any money or belongings, but they had each other.

Shortly after Mamawa moved to the United States in 1990, fighting intensified in a recently started civil war in Liberia, where rebel forces were overthrowing the government.

Her husband, Augustus, and the couple's three daughters "were caught between the enemy lines, in the crossfire. Wiande and her two sisters, my mother, and my husband had to flee the house with only what they had on, hands in the air, with soldiers and guns behind them," Mamawa said. "But God brought them through the toughest times of their lives."

They eventually made it to the United States, leaving behind a war that killed an estimated 200,000 people. Wiande, the oldest child, was seven years old, when the family settled in New York City.

"The Fulbright scholarship, that was God's way of bringing our family out of the civil war in Liberia," Mamawa said.

The family had to evacuate their home and find refuge. "My mother raised money and actually snuck back," said Wayetu Moore, one of Wiande's sisters.

While in New York, Mamawa was growing frantic. She had not been able to get in contact with her family for six months. Through a series of networks, she was able to hire a woman to find them and get them out of the small town in which they were hiding. Worried about her family's safety, Mamawa took a leave of absence from Columbia University and was able to be reunited with her family in Sierra Leone, which borders Liberia. Most Liberians went to Sierra Leone "to escape the brutal massacre that was going on as a result of the civil war," Mamawa said.

On February 14, 1991, the Moore family left Sierra Leone and headed to New York City. It was a joyous Valentine's Day for the reunited family. Mamawa was able to finish the semester at Columbia and earn her graduate degree.

The Moore family lived with Mamawa in student housing until the semester ended. They didn't have any money or belongings, but they had each other.

"Since everything we owned was on Liberian soil or in Liberian banks, my parents had to start over," said Wayetu, who has written a book about the journey, entitled, *These Legs Were Made for Walking*.

After Mamawa graduated from Columbia, the family moved to Connecticut for a few months, then lived in Tennessee for three years before establishing their roots in Texas in 1994.

Each move was driven by the search to reestablish a home and find steady jobs for a family that had grown to seven, including five children.

All of the experiences, which included the tragic killing of Wiande's grandfather in the war, strengthened the family's faith. And resolve.

Wiande displayed that resolve as she helped Kevin through an ordeal from hell.

"That was a devastating time for Wiande," said Mamawa, referring to the civil war and the death of Wiande's grandfather. "As little as Wiande was, she was being prepared to cope with Kevin's injury. She was only six years old, but had literally experienced a brutal civil war, a war that prepared her to handle life's most difficult blows. So when Kevin got injured, she was ready to be right there, by his side, being there with him through life's toughest times."

❖❖❖

During a break between rehab sessions, Kevin looked around the TIRR gym and felt fortunate. He saw patients in wheelchairs—some with one leg—who were struggling to gain their independence.

"He had a great attitude. He lifted my spirits."

Kevin sat down next to Wiande and put his uphill battle—*their* battle—in perspective.

"Kevin and I talked briefly about how many people in here are in a condition where they need assistance or are paralyzed and didn't get saved early enough, and therefore are a lot worse than what it's supposed to be," Wiande said. "I was telling him how I was talking to someone about her injury. She's paralyzed from the waist down for the rest of her life."

Kevin listened to the story and felt thankful he had come this far, thankful he had overcome the odds Dr. Cappuccino had set less than six weeks earlier: a 5 to 10 percent chance to walk.

As Kevin and Wiande talked, they noticed a young man about Kevin's age who was on a ventilator and paralyzed. After talking to some people in the gym, they learned that the man had suffered an injury similar to Kevin's.

Eight years ago.

Seeing the struggling young man gave Kevin and Wiande a strong dose of perspective.

❖ ❖ ❖

There were many old friends who visited with Kevin at TIRR, including his junior college coach at Kilgore, Jimmy Rieves. When Rieves arrived, Kevin was lying in bed and wearing a neck brace; he could lift his legs but still couldn't stand and couldn't move his arms or hands unless he was given assistance.

"He couldn't shake my hand," Rieves said.

Rieves lifted Kevin's spirits as he unfurled a huge get-well banner that players and fans from Kilgore and Navarro had signed. He also gave Kevin letters of encouragement that they had written.

After a few minutes of small talk, Rieves felt awkward as he tried to search for the right words to soothe his former player.

"I didn't know what to say. What do you say to someone after they're injured like that?" he asked.

Kevin sensed Rieves' discomfort.

"Coach, it's okay. Come on. I'm going to be all right," he said.

Rieves smiled at the memory.

"And from that very moment, I knew he was going to have a good recovery because of his attitude," he said. "He had a great attitude. He lifted *my* spirits."

Kevin mentioned to Rieves that his offseason training program helped make him mentally tough and prepared him for his current rehab. They talked about how two players from Kevin's Kilgore team—Thomas Herrion, who later played with the San Francisco 49ers, and Jake Jordan—had died tragically.

"He talked about those two guys and his injury…and how odd it was, and that we need to get together more often," Rieves said.

Rieves accompanied Kevin to the gym, where he went through some exercises. "I watched him work out, and his facial expressions reminded me of when he was in the weight room at Kilgore," Rieves said. "I knew he'd push himself."

❖ ❖ ❖

In October, Kevin's routine included sessions in TIRR's swimming pool, where he worked with rings and light wrist weights and did exercises to help strengthen his upper body. He also did leg exercises and felt exhausted when he was done.

Atkinson noticed that his patient began having the shades pulled up to let in the sunlight and that his light was turned on at night.

Eric Winston, Andre Davis, and Rashad Butler—three members of the NFL's Houston Texans—stopped by the hospital to spend time with Kevin. Winston and Butler had been Kevin's teammates at Miami. When the trio left, other friends and relatives visited. Kevin was a popular patient. The next day, Kevin received a phone call from his agent, informing him that NBC's Tiki Barber was in Houston and wanted to see him. Kevin said it wasn't the right time to talk to the media.

He had too much work to do and needed to stay focused.

It was almost as if Kevin now had tunnel vision: He was staring at a recovery for the ages—one that had created a new level of interest in the spinal-cord research community—and he didn't want anything to distract him from that mission.

Darryn Atkinson, the physical therapist, thought Kevin was on the road to recovery when he stopped keeping his hospital room dark. After Kevin's first few weeks at TIRR, Atkinson noticed that his patient began having the shades pulled up to let in the sunlight and that his light was turned on at night.

"After three full weeks of going in there every day and making a comment about it, it was cool to see him coming out of his shell," Atkinson said. "I went in there one day and the light was on, and the next day, even the shades were up on the windows. It was cool to see him kind of transition that way."

At about the same time, Kevin started to be less withdrawn at his weekly meetings with the TIRR medical team, said Worth Whiteside, the hospital's social worker.

Whiteside said there was a major change between Kevin's first meeting and the ones that followed a few weeks later. "There was a striking difference just in terms of Kevin's participation and his interaction with the team," Whiteside said. "I mean, I really sort of felt in the beginning he was still dealing with a whole bunch of stuff and getting used to being in the hospital, and in the first team rounds, he didn't have a lot to say. He was in a roomful of folks he hadn't known but a few days, and he was just a little bit more distant."

By the third week's meeting, Kevin was "very, very different," Whiteside said. "He was becoming more interactive. He began to show, I think, more who he really is, and his sense of humor started to come out, and to me, that's a significant thing."

Hearing Kevin crack jokes, Whiteside said, gave him a sense that his recovery was headed in the right direction.

"I once worked with a physician, a very wise physician, who said if you look back in time over a person's rehab course, in most cases you would see the point where they turned a corner and began to move forward," Whiteside said. "That trip could be a block or it could take 100 blocks, but the important thing was to be able to turn the corner; otherwise, you're stuck and can't go anywhere. I've been here many, many years and I've often thought about that, and I have looked back on many cases I've worked with—and you can almost see a point where people begin to move ahead. You can see that they're feeling better about themselves, they're feeling good about their progress, and for Kevin, I think it was probably within his second or third week of his hospital stay."

By early October, Kevin was comfortable in his surroundings—and with his team—at the Houston rehab hospital. His rapport with his therapists grew stronger each day, and after a few months at TIRR, he stunned one of them, Laredo, when they were talking about different languages they knew.

"He was telling me how he could write in Arabic, and I was really fascinated," Laredo said. "I had no idea that he knew any other language, let alone being able to write in that language. And so he said, 'Well, give me a pen and I'll show you.' At this point, it was just a regular old pen and not a built-up pen (that he used to need because it was easier to grasp), and he began to write."

Kevin sort of covered his work as he was writing; he didn't want to ruin the surprise. The end result was big block letters that said A-R-A-B-I-C, and in small letters embedded into it, he had printed K-E-V-I-N.

Get it? Kevin in Arabic.

It was a corny joke, but it showed Laredo that Kevin had come a long way from his early weeks at TIRR. He had emerged from his shell and was displaying the personality that his Buffalo Bills teammates knew and loved. He was smiling, connecting with people, happy to be alive.

In early October, Kevin's movements continued to improve. He was able to stand up for about a minute and a half on October 5, and he rode the exercise bike for nearly 10 minutes, though he was exhausted afterward.

Three days later, Kevin was able to stand for a total of five minutes, with a few breaks in between each stance. His feet appeared stronger than the previous week, when they looked "wiggly," Wiande said.

In the hospital that night, Kevin, Wiande, and several members of Wiande's family watched the Bills drop a heartbreaking 25–24 decision to the Dallas Cowboys, the team Kevin adored as a youngster.

"I don't even want to go into details about the game, I'm so sick right now," Wiande wrote in her journal, "but they played hard. I still love my Bills! We played very well."

The next day, October 9, would mark the one-month anniversary of Kevin's injury.

We woke up later today. We were both so tired. We got up at 9:30 AM. MRI at 10:45 AM. The nurses came in and did their normal routine. Medicines, breathing treatments and more meds.... After all the nurses left, it was time for OT (occupational therapy) with Rafferty, then outside to the Greenhouse with Dawn, and then Darryn (physical therapy). Today, with Dawn, we practiced with the cards again and Kevin did a great job. He worked his arms so well and his extension in his biceps/triceps is getting stronger. After Dawn, we met Darryn in the gym for PT. We worked on standing up again and he stretched Kevin really well. His MRI today was at 11:00 AM. We left TIRR with a security guard at 10:45 AM. His MRI went well. Kevin's progress is continuing to get better.

—Wiande's journal entry,
October 3, 2007

Little did Kevin, Wiande, and Patricia know that it was going to be a day for them to celebrate.

CHAPTER 8

FIRST STEPS (ADULT VERSION)

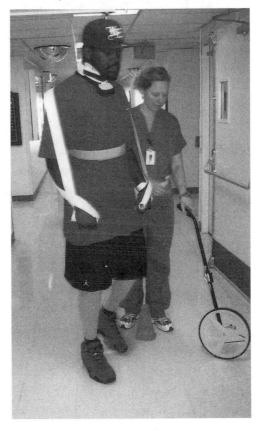

"I knew it was going to happen, no matter what the doctor said.
The doctor said he had a 5 percent chance
of ever walking again, but I know God
is a miracle worker and I knew he would walk again.
Kevin is a very hard worker and I knew this wasn't
going to stop him."

Back in 1983, Patricia Dugas was there to see her infant son's first steps.

Twenty-four years later, she got to see them again.

These steps were more gratifying. These steps came exactly one month after Kevin Everett's vicious collision on a football field.

Kevin Everett was paralyzed in front of millions on national TV.

Now, in the solitude of a Houston rehab center, in a tiny room with purple-painted bricks, adjacent to the gym, four others witnessed his first steps since his horrifying injury.

Never mind that he used a platform walker—one that had four wheels attached to it—to take the steps.

Never mind that a news crew wasn't there to document the magical moment.

Never mind that Kevin Everett wasn't an elite athlete anymore. He *was* a walking miracle.

Kevin had been reluctant to try to take some steps. He was still weak, and it made him nervous to be standing.

"We intended to just stand," said Darryn Atkinson, Kevin's physical therapist. "We didn't really stand up intending to take steps, but once he got comfortable with standing and was feeling good, he said he wanted to try it, so we tried it."

If Kevin grabbed onto the walker—which had a platform on it for his forearms—and lost his balance as he leaned on it, he could take off on an unwanted ride. So Atkinson held the walker to keep it steady.

Gingerly, Kevin took a small step, then another.

Patricia hadn't yet seen him stand, let alone take a step, in his rehab. As she watched Kevin take a few steps, her tear ducts emptied.

"He's walking! He's walking!" she shouted, clapping her hands as she followed her son around the room. *"My baby is walking!"*

Wiande began crying, too, but she turned her head and hid the tears from Kevin.

"I couldn't stop thanking God," she said. "I knew it was going to happen, no matter what the doctor said. The doctor said he had a 5 percent chance of ever walking again, but I know God is a miracle worker and I knew he would walk again. Kevin is a very hard worker and I knew this wasn't going to stop him."

Kevin had been reluctant to try to take some steps. He was still weak, and it made him nervous to be standing.

Seeing her 25-year-old son walk for the "first" time triggered memories for Patricia. Her mind drifted back to when Kevin was a baby and, as he wobbled across the room, she followed and made a diving scoop of her son before he hit the floor.

At the Houston hospital, she was still beside him, ready to catch him if he fell.

Kevin felt a sense of accomplishment but wasn't surprised he was able to take his first steps.

"I actually felt like it was something I was supposed to be doing," he said. "That's how I was feeling the whole time. I knew I would eventually get to this point, that it was just a matter of time, just a matter of hard work."

Seemingly reenergized, Kevin was able to increase the amount of steps he took on almost a daily basis.

Said Wiande: "He just has a positive attitude and the will and drive to do better each day."

That sounds very similar to what Kevin's football coaches have been saying. In high school, college, and the pros.

❖❖❖

"

Baby walked today with the walker. God is good. He walked 65 feet. The whole time he was walking, tears were in my eyes, but I made sure that he didn't see my tears. They were tears of joy, but I promised myself to not let Kevin see me cry. When he was in ICU, that was one thing, but this, this is God working and no one else through Kevin. God wants him to serve Him in something else in life. We were talking tonight about life in general and about some things he wants to do when he walks out of the hospital. He is truly determined, and every day I'm amazed by his work ethic and drive to get out of here 100 percent. I know by the grace of God, in his known time, he will.

—Wiande's journal entry,
October 9, 2007

"

Later in the week, Everett, in his first public comments since the injury, released a statement to fans through the Bills' public-relations department:

"I am deeply humbled by all of your support, your thoughts, and your prayers during this trying period in my life. As you may already be aware, I have shown significant progress in my recovery. But I am also fully aware that the recovery from this type of injury I have sustained is full of peaks and valleys. While the road to recovery is long and hard, I am determined to fight through it each and every day.

"This week, with the assistance of a walker, I was able to take steps, and I have been able to move in my wheelchair, both of which are great triumphs for me. I maintain a positive attitude and feel fortunate every day that I am alive and well. I value and appreciate the unfailing support of my family, my friends, my doctors, and my fans.

"While I am happy to share these moments of success in my recovery with you, I also ask that you understand this is a very challenging and personal time for me. I respectfully request that any future updates regarding my medical condition be obtained exclusively from the media relations team at Memorial

Hermann | TIRR. I hope that I can soon report another milestone in my recovery. Until then.

Respectfully,

Kevin Everett"

❖❖❖

When the NFL season started on September 9, Kevin weighed 255 pounds, but he was down to 216 pounds—39 pounds lighter—when he was weighed on October 7. He had been unable to eat solid food for a little over three weeks since his injury. "My right lung had shut down and my left lung wasn't working like it's supposed to," Everett explained, "so they didn't want me eating solid foods for a while because they could get trapped and I could start developing pneumonia. And then I kind of lost my appetite."

But the lung problem became resolved, and Kevin's appetite started to return. He was drinking Boost for energy, and Wiande was excited when he finished a bowl of Cap'n Crunch cereal for breakfast in early October. Soon, he was back to normal, eating chicken, shrimp, crawfish, pork chops, tacos, candied yams, cabbage, rice, potatoes, ice cream—even sandwiches from Subway.

With his renewed appetite and steady progress, doctors told Wiande that Kevin might be released as an inpatient on November 7. After that, he would continue to visit TIRR as a daily outpatient for an unforeseen amount of time.

At TIRR, Kevin and Wiande attended a class for spinal-cord patients. Kevin learned about breathing and how it is affected by his injury.

Wiande jotted down four pages of notes designed to help spinal-cord patients. When the class ended, Kevin and Wiande headed to his therapy sessions. Kevin, using a walker and working with Darryn Atkinson, was able to walk a little farther than the previous day. Kevin then used a toy football and an oversized gymnastic ball as he did drills with Dawn, working to improve his arms and legs and trying to strengthen his shoulders.

On October 22, Kevin was able to stand without assistance and able to walk with a regular walker, one that had just two wheels on the front. Kevin could do it under supervision, as opposed to assistance, where people held on to him to help keep his balance.

"

Kevin walked 440 feet today. He's doing so well! He said his feet are really tired. He gets so sleepy after PT (physical therapy) and OT (occupational therapy) that when he gets in the room, he's ready for a nap. I'm so proud of him and I know Mrs. Patricia is, too.

—Wiande's journal entry,
October 11, 2007

"

"He began getting less support from the therapists," Atkinson said. "He sort of started moving pretty quickly. Once he got up and going and the blood-pressure issues went away, that's really when he kind of took off."

As Kevin made strides, he became more connected with his therapists.

"When he started to make some recovery in his ability to stand and to walk or move his arms, he sort of came out of that (shell) and realized who we are," said Laredo, the occupational therapist. "Initially, we were just his therapists to him, and I think over the course of the rehab, certainly Darryn and I have become friends with Kevin and we're beyond the (early days), because we've experienced something really important in his life and we have been there."

He continued his grueling rehab schedule, doing squatting exercises until his neck started bothering him and he had to rest and lie on the floor. Atkinson, the physical therapist, explained to Kevin that the muscles in his neck and behind his skull get tight sometimes and need to be stretched. He also explained the importance of good posture and not getting to the point of straining the neck when Kevin wanted to see or sit.

Together, they did exercises to work on Kevin's deltoids and shoulder. Kevin's shoulder continued to ache. It didn't matter—he kept pushing.

By the end of October, Kevin was walking without any assistive device.

News of Kevin's accomplishments reached Buffalo, where the Bills were anxiously monitoring his progress.

"Every time I talk to him, he's saying, 'I'm moving this, I'm moving that,'" said Roscoe Parrish, a Bills wide receiver. "It's always something good that he's doing. Everybody is really proud of him because he could have just given up."

Many of the Bills phoned Kevin at the hospital for direct updates. Those who didn't call him received updates from Bills trainer Bud Carpenter, who was constantly in touch with Barbara Jackson, the case manager at TIRR.

The Bills would provide Jackson with authorization for activities out of TIRR, such as an MRI. Jackson was billing the Bills for Kevin's treatment and care.

Carpenter was excited when he read the reports Jackson sent to him. Team Kevin shared the joy.

"I remember when Kevin began getting his finger movement back and how thrilled we were to see it," said Dawn Brown, the TIRR recreational therapist. "He was not able to move objects, but he could work on pinching and picking up things. We began working on increasing strength, endurance, and fine-motor coordination by playing a variation of games that required more and more intricate abilities."

While Bills fans received dribs and drabs of information on Kevin's recovery, they didn't get a glimpse of the tight end until a surprising video was shown before Buffalo's Sunday night game against the powerful New England Patriots on November 18.

The Bills had sent someone to film Everett in his Humble, Texas, home. The 25-second video was shown on the Ralph Wilson Stadium scoreboard and on NBC before the game.

When Everett's image appeared, the sellout crowd cheered and then became silent.

"How ya doing, Buffalo? This is Kevin Everett," he said in the video as players from both sides and fans looked up at the scoreboard. "I'm out here in Houston, working hard out here, rehabbing, and I was just thinking about you guys."

The applause, which greeted Everett's image on the scoreboard, stopped completely. The stadium became church-quiet. The audience became captivated.

> *"It hurt bad, and he's not the first college teammate I've lost."*

"I just wanted to say thank you to all my teammates and the city of Buffalo, as well as the fans of America for all your support and love you've been giving me," Everett continued. "I just want to let you guys know that it's been special to me, and I just want to say, 'C'mon, let's beat New England.'"

The stadium went into a frenzy. Fans and players wiped their eyes. K.E. was in the house—at least his presence could be felt.

"We Love Kevin Everett," said a sign that a woman pumped high over her head. She seemed to be speaking for all of the 70,000-plus fans in the stadium.

Other than news releases, these were the first public comments made by Everett since his injury 10 weeks earlier.

Everett later admitted he hoped his message would inspire his teammates to a monumental upset. "I thought it would be some kind of boost of energy, you know," he said with a grin.

Instead, New England scored on its first seven possessions and

rolled to a 56–10 win. The Patriots' Tom Brady threw five touchdown passes—four to Randy Moss—as New England coasted
to the victory en route to finishing with a 16–0 regular-season
record.

At least the Buffalo fans had
one stirring memory from the
evening—and it was provided by
Everett, who earlier in the day had
been officially released from TIRR
as an inpatient—though he was still
rehabbing five days a week at the
hospital as an outpatient.

When Everett's image appeared, the sellout crowd cheered and then became silent.

❖ ❖ ❖

In late November, the NFL was rocked by the death of Washington Redskins All-Pro safety Sean Taylor, who was shot by an
intruder at his luxurious home in Palmetto Bay, Florida. A bullet
severed a major artery in his thigh, causing a fatal loss of blood.

The news was especially difficult for Kevin and Wiande,
each of whom attended the University of Miami with Taylor and
became friendly with him.

"This is so shocking because it seems like just the other
day we were in English class at Miami, laughing and clowning
around," Wiande said.

"It hurt bad, and he's not the first college teammate I've lost,"
Kevin said. He wanted to attend Taylor's funeral services, "but I
was unable to go because I had these issues going on with me
and had to go see my doctors."

In her journal entry on November 29—two days after Taylor
died—Wiande wrote: "Today, I just kept thinking about the
incident with Sean and how life is truly short. You have to live
your life to the fullest and make sure that you know where you're
going when you die. My heart goes out to his family and his

mother. I just went through this two months ago with Kevin, so I know how it feels to see someone you love in bed and not able to know or acknowledge that you are here."

Five days after Taylor's death, the Redskins dropped a 17–16 decision to the visiting Bills on December 2. Buffalo won it when Rian Lindell kicked a 36-yard field goal—after a 15-yard Washington penalty for an illegal timeout—with four seconds left.

"It makes your heart drop all the way to your feet," Redskins quarterback Jason Campbell said. "We wanted to come back here and win one for Sean."

When the Redskins' defense came out onto the field for the first time, Taylor's safety position was left vacant in a tribute to their friend. Only 10 players were on the field for Fred Jackson's 22-yard run around left end.

It was great to be walking again, great to feel a part of the festive season, great to be able to get pleasure out of such an everyday event—strolling through a mall.

"It was a very emotional day for everybody," Bills coach Dick Jauron said. "I'm sure more so for them, but we have a number of players on our squad that were very close to Sean, played with him in college or the NFL. I thought both teams would play hard, and that would honor him. That's how he played the game. He played it all out. It was a 60-minute game; that's how he played.

"It's unfortunate," Jauron added, "that one of these teams had to lose this day."

Earlier in the week, Pedro Taylor, Sean's father, had addressed the Redskins and urged them to win their final five games and make the playoffs. They answered one of his requests.

After the excruciating loss to Buffalo, the Redskins won their last four games, finished 9–7 and earned a wild-card playoff berth. Sean Taylor was their inspiration.

❖ ❖ ❖

Six nights before Christmas, Kevin and Wiande strolled through an upscale Houston mall, the nationally renowned Galleria, to do some last-minute shopping for a trip to Buffalo, where the Bills were playing their final home game of an uneasy season. Kevin, wearing a tan sweat suit and a neck brace, was recognized by a handful of people, including one man who gave him a gentle hug. "You look great. You look like you're almost all the way back," he told Kevin.

It had been a busy day for Everett. Five hours of rehab with Team Kevin at TIRR, including 45 minutes in the pool. Lunch with Wiande, workout-buddy Virgil, and his wife, Lyn, at Luby's, a cafeteria-style restaurant in Houston. And lots of errands: a haircut with Pat Williams, Kevin's barber; a visit with front-office executives of Houston's professional women's basketball team (Kevin bought some season tickets to the Comets' WNBA games and planned to let his sisters use lots of them); and a return trip to the rehab center to pick up Lyn's homemade lemon cheesecake, which Kevin had accidentally left behind.

Now, as a Bing Crosby Christmas tune serenaded shoppers through the mall's loudspeakers, they walked around the Galleria to find a winter coat that Wiande could take to Buffalo, home of temperatures that would make a Texan shiver.

Kevin was enjoying himself. It was great to be walking again, great to feel a part of the festive season, great to be able to get pleasure out of such an everyday event—strolling through a mall.

Holding Wiande's hand as he walked, Kevin spotted a coat he thought she would like as they went past the window of United Colors of Benetton.

It turned out he was right. Wiande bought a stylish black

wool coat, along with a brown leather jacket. As she paid for the purchases, the petite-sized saleswoman glanced up at the 6'4" Everett.

"You *must* play basketball," she said.

Kevin, playfully massaging Wiande's shoulders, smiled.

He's a football player, the saleswoman was told.

She had no idea that Kevin had been in the NFL, no idea of his injury, of his movie-like recovery.

"Football? I must be too old. I don't understand football," she said.

"It's easy," Kevin deadpanned. "Just give me the ball and watch me score."

The woman chuckled, not realizing the irony in Kevin's off-the-cuff remark. He had talked about football in the present tense, as if it was still the sport he played.

Kevin still had a way to go before he was totally independent in his daily life. But if he did regain his independence, was there even a slight chance he could return to playing in the NFL?

At present, doctors said absolutely no. End of story. And Kevin seemed resigned that he would never play again. Dr. Teodoro Castillo, his attending physician at TIRR in Houston, said Kevin may not be able to run again, let alone play in the NFL.

"It remains to be seen" if Kevin can ever run, Castillo said. "I think he will, based on what I see right now. The question now is…looking at the more fine details, like making sure he doesn't have what we call *proprioception*. When we're standing, we know where our feet are positioned. That's why we keep our balance. So that's the thing we're trying to focus on."

Kevin still doesn't have that balance; in time and with lots of therapy, the hope is that he will regain it, the doctor said.

"That's the thing we're going to try to focus on," he said. "Obviously, the faster you walk, you have to make sure your balance is really great, and they're still working on his trunk muscles" to regain that ability.

In other words, Kevin had to learn how to walk fast before he could even think about running. And that was a goal that was far down the road.

"We have a gait trainer here, so most likely he would go through that, where his body is supported and he's on the treadmill," Castillo said.

Castillo was asked if he thought Kevin's miraculous recovery would continue and enable him to play in the NFL again.

"Oh, gosh, that's a tough question to answer," he said with a smile. "Right now, I think he's showing me so many good things that I would kind of really defer answering that. I don't know if it's fair to do that because I see them (patients), then I reassess each time and then we see…where we are at each point. At this point, right now, obviously not."

It seemed as if Castillo didn't want to shut the door on the possibility, however slight.

"Well, you have to think of the whole picture," he said. "Will he be at 100 percent? I don't know how close to 100 percent he'll be as he continues his recovery phase. And with the risk— football, as you know, is a contact sport—and even if you stabilize somebody, it's going to be a very big decision to go back, even if he regained 100 percent.

"So I think for now, definitely at this point, the answer is no."

Castillo will be reassessing Kevin and his ever-changing condition in the following weeks and months—and perhaps years.

"We usually wait for a lot of our patients who have incomplete (spinal injuries) a year, a year and a half, and sometimes even two years to see how much you did recover," he said, "and the longer you are from the injury, the chances that he won't get most of it back is going to be great."

Castillo was referring to the return of Kevin's sensory skills, motor skills, and balance.

"The highest expectation of recovery is Day One of the injury to the first year," he said, "so let's say as an example, Kevin or somebody else, recovers 50 percent of what he lost. In the second year...the chance of getting 50 percent again would be very small. It's going to be smaller as you go further away from the injury."

By late December, Kevin had been able to do activities needed in daily living, such as feeding, dressing, and washing himself. He had tone deficiencies in his right arm and right hand—it was still a challenge for him to write his name—that the therapists were working to improve. The motor skills still needed lots of fine-tuning before Kevin could drive a car again and perform some other important tasks.

As far as basic physical skills needed in everyday life, "Kevin has no limitations, but he may be doing things a lot slower than he used to," Castillo said.

For instance, if it had taken him 10 seconds to put on a shirt before the injury, it might take him twice as long—or more—in his present condition.

"He doesn't require any assisted devices to do any of these self-care needs," the doctor said, "so I think he's doing everything now on his own, but it probably takes a bit longer to do it."

Kevin was able to walk on his own for at least an hour, and he did it at a steady pace. The medical staff at TIRR was hopeful he would be able to increase his walking speed down the road.

"We want to make him more efficient with his gait, with his gait pattern," Castillo said. "It's a lot more fine-tuning, making sure that his balance—proprioception—is back. And then we challenge him again."

So far, Kevin had answered every challenge Castillo and his staff had presented.

"That's why I admire Kevin so much," Castillo said. "When I first spoke to his mom when Kevin first got here, she told me Kevin is such a focused guy in terms of when he was in the NFL. Every morning he would be up at 6 and focus on his training. He would wake up at 6 and run; he was on a rigid schedule."

That schedule helped prepare him for the workouts and rehab exercises supervised by Team Kevin.

By late December, Kevin had been able to do activities needed in daily living, such as feeding, dressing, and washing himself.

"I told Kevin that I actually see all my patients as athletes because all my patients have weaker muscles but they have to accomplish some goals," Castillo said. "He already knew about the challenge" that accompanies rehabilitation. "He's doing a great job. He's always focused.

"The biggest part of the problem now that I'm anticipating... depends on what Kevin's definition of normal is. Of course you aim for 100 percent normal, but..."

That doesn't always happen.

For some patients, the recovery Kevin has experienced is great, "but some patients may have a higher expectation," Castillo said.

❖ ❖ ❖

Like he did with his football team, Kevin built many relationships at Memorial Hermann | TIRR with the doctors, therapists, and patients. Those relationships were still building in late November—especially with his therapists—even though he was now an outpatient at the hospital.

The therapists, particularly Laredo and Atkinson, had developed a chemistry with Kevin, one that blended perfectly with his single-minded focus.

From September through the beginning of 2008, the therapists fed off Kevin's focus and helped push him to the highest possible recovery. Kevin approached his rehab sessions with an intensity that had become his trademark—his calling card—in high school, college, and the NFL.

The therapists—Rafferty Laredo, Darryn Atkinson, Dawn Brown, and Liza Criswell—became his coaches. Much like Bills coach Dick Jauron and his huge staff.

"Darryn, Rafferty, Dawn, and Liza were very good to me and easy to work with," Kevin said. "When I first got to TIRR, they set up a plan and they said we were going to get it done—and we did. They didn't want me to cheat myself."

Kevin's fellow patients, his new teammates, also pushed him.

When he was released as an inpatient at TIRR, Kevin issued a statement that praised the "extraordinary people" he had met at the hospital, including "many who have suffered the same injury as myself, many of whom I now consider friends. Their courage and determination inspired me every day in my recovery to walk.

Switching to an outpatient meant Kevin could live in the beautiful two-story house he had purchased for his family.

"To my fans: Thank you for your loyalty," he said. "To my doctors and physical therapists: Thank you for keeping me healthy and strong. To my friends and family: Thank you for your unwavering love and support. Until next time."

In the statement, alluding to his release from the hospital as an outpatient, Kevin added, "While this news is a significant milestone for me, I still have a long journey to full recovery."

Laredo agreed. The occupational therapist said Kevin's transition to an outpatient "only means he no longer needs the attention of inpatient nursing and physician contact on a daily basis."

Now Kevin's rehabilitation needs were met by working primarily with the occupational therapist and physical therapist. He was making progress but still needed lots of fine-tuning with his arms, hands, and legs.

Switching to an outpatient meant Kevin could live in the beautiful two-story house he had purchased for his family in Humble, located about 35 minutes from the Houston hospital. It would be good to be back home, good to be with his mom and three sisters, good to taste his mom's cooking.

Wiande would drive Kevin to rehab each weekday morning; he would be an outpatient for an undetermined amount of time.

Castillo called Everett's progress "the most significant recovery" of all the central-cord patients he has treated in his 12 years of practice. Central-cord syndrome is a condition in which patients with spinal-cord injuries display weaker upper extremities than lower extremities.

Kevin fit in that class.

"Kevin definitely had the central-cord picture because when he came here, he barely could move his arms, but he could move his legs," Castillo said. "Considering where he came from on Day One, I'm very happy with the way he's progressed. He went from not being able to move his arms (much) to where he can stand, walk, and do his self-care with little assistance."

Castillo said he has treated "hundreds" of cases similar to Kevin's.

"A lot of patients that I've seen, a majority of them really don't get a lot of hand recovery, as much as Kevin did. So a lot of them will require an assistive device in order for them to eat and do their hygiene, but Kevin was able to progress to the point that he's able to do it—but not obviously at 100 percent—without an assistive device."

Castillo credited Kevin's care at the scene of the injury for triggering his recovery.

"He got stabilized really quick. They basically immobilized him at the scene, transported him to the medical center in a very quick time, and basically decompressed his neck. They did the assessment and they said, 'We have to decompress the neck and they did it.'"

Had Kevin's recovery gone beyond everyone's expectations? That was the question posed to Dr. William Donovan, the hospital's medical director.

"I'm gratified, but, no, I'm not surprised because we take each individual injury as a unique case unto itself and make the best of what we can," Donovan said. "In other words, if the person gets recovery, we take advantage of that recovery by offering more challenges; we want to take it to the next level, all the way, which is what he wants, too. So we do push them, but only as far as what we can expect."

❖ ❖ ❖

A few days before his return to Buffalo for the first time since his injury, Kevin was happy at the chance to be reunited with his teammates. It would also be a draining time, he realized, because he knew he would never be their teammate again.

Kevin planned to meet with the Bills before their home finale against the New York Giants.

"It's going to be very emotional, to be quite honest," he said. "I mean, that's what I do. I play football. And before the injury at that place.... It's going to be a very sad feeling for me, but happy at the same time. Just to be back with my teammates. They're guys that I've grown to love and enjoyed being around. To see their faces, that's going to be the most emotional part of it. I know they're going to rally around me because...it may sound silly, but I had a relationship with all the guys on the team, believe it or not. I was established with each and every one of them. I wouldn't shy myself from anyone on the team. I wanted to be associated with everybody, because you know there's much more than football. At the end of the day, we're all grown men."

He may have had a difficult time in English class in high school, but Kevin had grown into an expert communicator.

"It's kind of hard to actually meet 60-some guys on the team, hard to meet each and every one of them and get a feel for each one," he said. "I try to at least introduce myself to everybody. Little conversations. It doesn't have to be much. We could be watching TV together and a guy I never talked to is sitting next to me. I just start talking to him and he tells me his name and we start."

Building relationships is more important to Kevin than the average pro athlete. He is sensitive, introspective, and, like his grandfather, a people person. Some people have described him as quiet, but that couldn't be further from the truth.

"It's going to be very emotional, to be quite honest."

Soft-spoken, yes. Quiet, no. He has a dry, quick-witted sense of humor and a knack for making folks feel comfortable in his company.

"People gravitate toward him," Wiande said.

He has the unique ability to fit into almost any social group.

"He has a personality for everybody," said Paul Lancaster, the Bills' executive who had to phone Kevin's mom on that dreadful September day and tell her to quickly travel to Buffalo. "I've seen him be introspective and quiet, and I've seen him be the other guy, where he's joking back and forth and outgoing."

Serious Kevin. Comical Kevin. Heroic Kevin.

Wiande loved each one.

CHAPTER 9

A CHRISTMAS GIFT:
THE RETURN TO BUFFALO

"Seeing them looking at me, they couldn't believe it; they were just

so happy and it was a great feeling,

I can't even lie about it. It was emotional.

I had to hold back the tears.

When I saw them, I wanted to suit up

and go back on the field."

It was emotional and, at the same time, a little eerie, this return to Buffalo, this home-for-the-holidays reunion with his Buffalo Bills teammates, this return to The House That Hosted a Career-Ending Injury.

But there Kevin Everett was, back at Ralph Wilson Stadium, when the Bills played their final home game of the season against the New York Giants on December 23, 2007.

> *"Every time I watch the film, with the return we were running, I keep thinking, 'You were supposed to be blocked.'"*

Contributing to the eeriness was the fact that Domenik Hixon, the Denver Broncos player who collided with Everett when he suffered his near-fatal injury three and a half months earlier, was now a member of the Giants.

From the second he entered blustery Ralph Wilson Stadium for the second time this season, Hixon felt uneasy. "The surroundings, the locker room, everything was the same," he said. "You have a job to do out there. You try to put it out of your mind, but that's not easy."

Hixon remembered the tackle, which initially left Everett paralyzed from the neck down, as one of the hardest hits he had ever absorbed on a football field. "Even when I was getting up, I was dazed and my shoulder felt funny," he said. "One of my teammates said, 'He's not getting up.' I turned around and when they brought the ambulance out, I was hoping it was more precautionary than anything else."

Everett said he had no hard feelings toward Hixon.

"Not at all," he said. "I don't see why I should feel any anger or resentment toward him. You know, he didn't mean it. He didn't intentionally lower his helmet or shoulder...to try to break my neck. Who knew it was going to happen?"

"I've been praying about it every day, hoping and wishing for the best," Hixon said. "From what I've been hearing, he has a little bit to go, but it's very exciting that he's making progress."

The injury occurred in the teams' season opener, when Hixon was tackled by Everett on the second-half kickoff. A second-year wide receiver from Akron, Hixon said it was difficult to deal with the situation.

"Even when I went home and saw it on TV, I still couldn't believe it," he said. "After a couple of days, it really hit me that it happened."

Hixon played three more games with Denver before getting waived and finished with mediocre averages in kickoff (22.8 yards) and punt (4.6) returns.

The collision with Everett affected his play, Hixon said, after watching films of his returns.

"I looked at the way I played after it happened, and that wasn't me. It's not how I play," he said. "I was trying not to let it affect me, but it did, just the way I ran the ball. I looked tentative, like I was second-guessing every time."

Everett's injury was a freak accident, but friends and relatives had a difficult time convincing Hixon. He talked with his family, his pastor, his coaches, teammates, and friends. All told him the injury wasn't his fault.

But Hixon couldn't get a certain thought out of his mind: The collision had forever changed Everett's life.

"You've got to understand that God has a plan," a friend told Hixon.

Hixon had watched a replay of the collision. Over and over and over.

"Every time I watch the film, with the return we were running, I keep thinking, 'You were supposed to be blocked,'" said Hixon, referring to Everett.

Hixon is one of Everett's biggest fans; he has been following his progress at TIRR in Houston.

"It's good to see how well he's done," he said. "I remember talking to my parents afterward and they were praying for him. They told me to pray for him. That's just how God works."

"If you look at it, it's really a walking miracle because he was so close to not walking again or not even making it," Bills safety Donte Whitner said. "And now he's walking a couple months later. That's a miracle in itself when doctors were saying, 'We don't know if Kevin's going to do this.'"

❖ ❖ ❖

The last time he was here, he was being whisked away on an ambulance and doctors thought he would be paralyzed. Or worse. Now, less than four months later, he had returned as the conquering hero.

Fans held signs around the stadium: "Welcome Back Kevin Everett," said one. "God Bless 85" and "We Love Kevin Everett," said others.

Someone in a Santa Claus suit held up a banner that captured the atmosphere of the day:

Bills Tickets: $150.

Parking: $50.

Kevin Everett Walking: Priceless.

"I got to hug him. That's good for the heart."

Everett addressed his Bills teammates—some of whom had last seen him lying in a hospital bed in Buffalo, heavily sedated—about two hours before their December 23 game against the Giants. One of Everett's goals was to return to Buffalo for the Bills' final home game of the season.

"I was speechless, on the verge of tears," Buffalo rookie quarterback Trent Edwards said. "He got out of his wheelchair and had a smile on his face. I remember the last time I saw him, he was out there on the field with his head down, getting an ambulance, and we were all gathering around saying a prayer for him."

Those prayers, apparently, were answered.

Everett went from locker to locker before the game and talked with each of his teammates. He also shared a pregame meal with them.

"It seemed like nothing had even happened to him," Bills linebacker John DiGiorgio said. "He was standing up, smiling. He gave me a hug and everything. It helped me and all the guys on the team."

Edwards couldn't contain his glee—and surprise—at how much progress Kevin had made.

"The last time I saw him on this field, it was a pretty devastating sight," he said.

Edwards was teary-eyed as he watched Kevin make his away around the locker room before the game and spend time with his teammates.

"I couldn't stop looking at him," Edwards said. "It's very remarkable, and I'm not surprised that a guy that strong can get through an injury like that, both physically and mentally. That says a lot about the individual he is."

"I got to hug him," Bills running back Marshawn Lynch said. "That's good for the heart."

"You could see guys wiping their eyes as they met him at the pregame meal," Bills general manager Marv Levy said. "It was very emotional thing seeing him back with the team. I think it was very beneficial for the team and for Kevin. He's meant a lot to our team, and everyone is just so happy about what's going on with him."

Some of the Bills approached Everett and shook hands but

appeared concerned about not being too physical with him, Levy said.

"Kevin would shake hands and then say, 'Hey, how about a big hug?' and then the players would hug him," Levy said. "It was a moving scene."

"He's battled, he's scrapped, he's hung in there tough because he always had a good spirit about it," said Bobby April, Buffalo's assistant head coach. "It's just awesome to see someone overcome obstacles."

Everett—who was also reunited with the Bills' medical staff, including Andrew Cappuccino, the orthopedist who put his recovery in motion—asked teammate John McCargo to visit him in Houston, where he is continuing his rehab.

"It makes you believe there really is a God," said McCargo, the Bills' 6'2", 301-pound defensive tackle from Drakes Branch, Virginia. "Three and a half months ago, he couldn't move anything, and it just makes my day to see him walking. I'm definitely going to go down and chill with him."

The return of Everett was an early Christmas present for those associated with the Bills—and for all of the NFL.

"He touched everyone's heart," Buffalo wide receiver Lee Evans said.

"It was absolutely a great gift to see Kevin and to have him back with our football team," Bills coach Dick Jauron said. "He's been a part of our team—and will continue to be a part of our team—and to be able to see him and look him in the eye and shake his hand, it's hard to describe what it means to all of us and how lucky we feel to have it going like this."

On ESPN that night, broadcaster Chris Berman proclaimed: "We saw Kevin Everett walk today and (that means) we know that Santa Claus is coming to town."

"It's Buffalo's Christmas gift," said Roscoe Parrish, one of the

Bills' wide receivers.

Bills tight end Robert Royal shook his head when he said Kevin was "doing the same thing we're all doing...and that's an amazing thing. He couldn't stand for a long period of time, but he was up for about an hour, hour and a half on his own today and walking around. God has touched him."

Kevin playfully poked fun at his teammates, who dished it right back at him. He seemed like the same old Kevin, the guy who loved playing practical jokes.

"That's just the kind of guy he is and that's the kind of bond we have," said Parrish, who was also Kevin's teammate at the University of Miami.

After meeting with his teammates before the game, Kevin left the locker room in a wheelchair and, on his own power, climbed into a covered electric golf cart. He was driven to team president Ralph Wilson's midfield suite—fans and concessionaire workers applauded him on his way there—and he watched the game with Wiande and his family and friends by his side. Patricia was there, too, along with Kevin's three sisters, his future mother-in-law, Mamawa Moore, and his good friend Tony Tompkins, the one-time tiny quarterback whom Kevin had kiddingly ridiculed back in eighth grade.

Seemingly inspired by Everett's presence, the Bills jumped out to a 14–0 first-quarter lead. Buffalo held a 21–17 lead in the fourth quarter before the Giants rallied and defeated the Bills, 38–21, in nasty conditions that included rain, wind, and snow.

After the game, Hixon met with Everett in a suite upstairs in the stadium.

"He looked great," Hixon said. "We just had some casual conversation. We talked a little bit about everything. I won't necessarily say it brought 100 percent closure. I just want to see him get better."

When Kevin and Hixon met, neither mentioned their collision. "We didn't talk about what happened or what we've been going through," Kevin said. "It was just a meet and greet. I said hello and told him I was doing well. I told him I wanted to meet him earlier, but, due to my circumstances at the rehab, it couldn't happen. It was just a casual conversation and he seemed very laid back and like a real cool guy."

"It's a blessing," Hixon said of Everett's improving condition. "I just want him to make a 100 percent recovery. I'm going to continue praying for him, and he's going to make it back 100 percent."

After visiting with Hixon, Kevin and his entourage went to a nearby restaurant before the group took a plane back to Texas.

Patricia called it a "beautiful" trip. "We lost, but it was still OK," she said. "We enjoyed the game and being with his teammates."

"Everybody was hugging everybody," Patricia said.

Everett, who the previous month was filmed at home and had his statement broadcast before Buffalo's home game against New England, was not available for interviews and did not go on the field to address the fans during halftime. Winds were already gusting at more than 30 miles per hour, and there was a persistent drizzle falling two hours before kickoff. The drizzle changed to an icy, wind-driven snow during the game.

It would have been dangerous for Kevin to walk under those conditions, but he said the purpose of the trip wasn't to walk on the field—that moment may arrive in the future—but to be reunited with his teammates and coaches.

"I wanted to watch the last home game and wanted to be there with my teammates, that was the intention," said Kevin, who was worn out from walking around the airport the previous day and sat in a wheelchair while at Ralph Wilson Stadium. "I just wanted to lay low and be with my guys. It was a great feeling to be reunited with my guys after being with them every day for a long time."

Many had not seen him since the injury and were stunned by how well he was able to move.

"Seeing them looking at me, they couldn't believe it; they were just so happy and it was a great feeling, I can't even lie about it," Kevin said. "It was emotional. I had to hold back the tears. When I saw them, I wanted to suit up and go back on the field."

Kevin said he was surprised to see so many new faces in the locker room. The Bills had 15 players on injured reserve, including Everett, causing the team to have a different look.

"There were guys I had never seen before," Kevin said. "It was like I was in a foreign land."

But it wasn't foreign. It was the place where he had caught his first NFL pass in 2006 and his last one in 2007; it was the place where his career ended in the blink of an eye, the place where he hopes to return for the 2008 home opener and walk on the field to inspire the Bills to a season worth remembering.

❖ ❖ ❖

Wiande's journal entry after the Buffalo trip was much longer than usual:

"We arrived in Buffalo at 10:00 PM on December 22. The next day was the Bills vs. Giants game. (Kevin's first game back to Buffalo since his injury on September 9.) We woke up early in the morning to head to the facility for Kevin to see his teammates and coaches. Paul Lancaster drove me, my mother, and Kevin to the facility and we went to the tight-end room to Kevin's coach, Coach (Charlie) Coiner. On our way, we met with Coach Dick Jauron (Kevin's head coach) and he was so excited to see Kevin back healthy and able to move around that he just couldn't stop smiling and hugging Kevin.

"When we arrived in the room, Kevin said, 'This is where I

used to put in my long hours of work after practice.' He sat in the chair where he used to sit and began telling us about what he used to do in the film room and showed us how and what they did while watching film.

"Behind him, on the back wall, was a bulletin board with his football picture and the caption 'Warrior: Keep Fighting.' I looked at him and smiled because he truly is a warrior in my eyes and in others all around the world. We (proceeded) to the cafeteria, where Kevin met with his teammates and coaches. The first person that Kevin saw was a young lady who works in the cafeteria. She immediately dropped the utensils she carried in her hand and grabbed a hold of Kevin. 'Awww, sweetie,' she said. 'I'm so happy to see you.... Look at this!' She started crying. Then she looked at me and said, 'Thank you.' She didn't have to explain herself because I knew what she meant. She hugged me and then Mrs. Patricia, and Kevin's sisters walked in the cafeteria to greet and say hello to all of the players that came in. When we were seated at the table, the young lady continued to come by our table and ask if we were OK and if we needed anything. Then she asked Kevin, 'Do you want me to make you anything, hon?' Kevin said, 'The usual.' The usual was a bacon, egg-white, and cheese sandwich.

"The game started great and the Bills were up 14–0. I knew that it had a lot to do with Kevin's presence."

"Kevin continued to chat with teammates like Robert Royal, Ryan Neufeld, Josh Reed, Roscoe Parrish, and many others. The guys had to go to the locker room and get ready for the game so we headed to the box to watch the game. While sitting in the box, fans glanced and smiled while some fans knocked on the window to tell Kevin hello. One fan had a Santa Claus suit on and he came to the window with a huge banner that said: 'Bills Tickets: $150. Parking: $50. Kevin Everett Walking: Priceless.' We all smiled and watched as Kevin thanked the man with a thumbs-up.

"Before the game started, Kevin predicted the score to be Bills 50, Giants 14. Mr. Wilson (Ralph Wilson, the team president) and his wife came by the box to see Kevin, Mrs. Patricia and me, and the rest of the family. Then they left to go watch the game. When they left, I continued to see fans with Kevin Everett T-shirts and jerseys on. My eyes watered. The game started great and the Bills were up 14–0. I knew that it had a lot to do with Kevin's presence. His teammates love him so much!

"Then...Buffalo weather began to take over and it started pouring down rain and at the same time it started snowing really bad. I looked over at Kevin's face. He was focused. His eyes were on the game and on his teammates. He screamed, 'Let's go, 'Scoe!' (Roscoe's nickname) and, 'Come on, Rob!' (Robert Royal). The score was now tied in the second quarter and then the game went downhill. We all continued to scream and cheer on the Bills, but you know some fans just don't cheer when the team is doing bad. They only cheer when the team is winning! I remember back in college at the University of Miami when Kevin was playing, Miami fans would act the same way. If Miami was down and not winning at that very moment, they would give up on the team. I never understood that. I love football (sports in general) and I'm a very optimistic person, so I always scream really loud at games, and even at home when no one's watching. I know how to motivate others around me to get fired up for the game. I said, 'Let's Go Buffalo!' When I said this, everyone in the box started screaming, including Davia, Kevin's youngest sister (whom we call Tinka) sitting next to me.

"We all hoped for the best and so did Kevin. He hates to lose and when he saw the final score of the game, he was down but at the same time he was happy because he saw his teammates play. He saw them play the game of football that he loves so dearly and will always love for the rest of his life. He saw the field he once played and practiced on. He stared at the Ralph Wilson Stadium, where people once watched his number 85 handle the ball and run around the field, and he smiled. He smiled because, though he's not playing that role anymore as an NFL star, he's still a star in the eyes of his family, teammates, and fans all over the world. They will always be watching and waiting to see what lies ahead for Kevin Everett."

❖❖❖

Forget *It's a Wonderful Life* and *Miracle on 34th Street*. All around the country, Kevin Everett's recovery and return to Buffalo was the feel-good story of the Christmas season.

Nike took out a full-page ad in the *Buffalo News*, saluting Kevin's triumphant return. The ad read: "9/9/07 Kevin Everett is carted off the field with a spinal cord injury. 9/10/07 Medical experts say there's only a 5–10 % chance that he will ever walk again. 12/23/07 Kevin walks back onto the field today."

America needed an uplifting sports story. Kevin Everett provided it.

In his blog for the *Baltimore Sun*, under the headline "Everett's recovery worthy of a holiday miracle," Bill Ordine wrote: "Kevin Everett, the Buffalo Bills' tight end who suffered that frightening spinal-cord injury in the first game of the season against Denver, was back at Ralph Wilson Stadium yesterday and walked into the Bills' locker room.

"…That the injured player was able to travel from Houston, where he has been rehabilitating, and meet and talk with his teammates and have a pregame meal with them…is truly a miracle worthy of the season.

A CHRISTMAS GIFT: THE RETURN TO BUFFALO

"...While a Buffalo triumph would have been a nice Christmas present for Everett, his own victory—being able to walk into the locker room—looms larger than any numbers on a scoreboard. "And regardless of who lifts the Vince Lombardi Trophy in February, I think it's fair to say that Kevin Everett can be considered the biggest winner of this NFL season."

In *USA Today*, Christine Brennan called Everett's recovery "perhaps the happiest moment of the year in sports." She wrote about how Kevin, paralyzed after his September 9 tackle, was now moving, and she ended her piece with this: "Talk about your wonderful sports upsets."

A black cloud seemingly hung over the sports world in 2007. There was disgraced former NBA referee Tim Donaghy admitting he bet on games he worked—and that he tipped off gamblers with inside information on which teams to bet on. There was track star Marion Jones, after years of angry denials, revealing she took steroids before winning five medals at the 2000 Summer Olympics. There was the daily debate about whether Barry Bonds should have an asterisk placed next to his home-run record because of steroid use.

There was the steroid scandal that rocked Major League Baseball, former Atlanta Falcons quarterback Michael Vick receiving a prison sentence for his role in a dog-fighting ring, and the Tennessee Titans' Adam "Pacman" Jones being suspended from the NFL for the 2007 season for numerous violations of the league's personal conduct policy, including 10 incidents in which he was interviewed by police. One of the incidents involved a fight and shooting at a Las Vegas strip club that left a man paralyzed.

In short, America needed an uplifting sports story.

Kevin Everett provided it. And it was touching people from all around the country, whether they were sports fans or not.

❖ ❖ ❖

Kevin's recovery put him on the cover of the December 17 issue of *Sports Illustrated*, accompanied by the headline, "Against All Odds: Kevin Everett Is Walking Again." Inside, nine pages were devoted to Kevin's recovery.

He had become a national phenomenon.

But folks in Port Arthur, Texas, already knew that their native son was somebody special, that he never forgot his roots, that he took pride in making improvements to the city.

Kevin's giving nature was demonstrated when he hosted a free one-day football camp last summer for young players at his high school alma mater, which used to be called Thomas Jefferson but is now Memorial. Young players from what is known as the Golden Triangle—Port Arthur, Orange, and Beaumont—attended the clinic. In addition to Kevin, several NFL players served as clinicians, including the Pittsburgh Steelers' Casey Hampton, the Jacksonville Jaguars' Brian Iwuh, the Green Bay Packers' Michael Montgomery and Johnny Jolly, the Minnesota Vikings' Robert Ferguson and Cedric Griffin, and the Cleveland Browns' Lawrence Vickers.

"I wanted to give back to my community, because when I was a kid, we didn't have anyone who would come back."

The NFL players and some local high school coaches ran drills, along with Michael Sims, who helped organize the Kevin Everett Foundation Youth Camp.

Kevin had wanted to run a camp before his rookie season with the Bills, but his representative, Eric Armstead, advised against it "because you need a year to learn the offense and it's your make-or-break year."

Armstead wasn't one of those cutthroat types who negotiated a contract but had little contact with his client. He and Kevin were close. They socialized and frequently exchanged ideas and phone calls. During Kevin's second season with the Bills, he and Armstead discussed plans that made the camp a reality in the summer before Kevin's third NFL season.

"I wanted to give back to my community, because when I was a kid, we didn't have anyone who would come back," Everett said. "That's the least I could do."

Besides a day of counseling from NFL players, campers were given T-shirts, sneakers or cleats, and lunch. Wal-Mart donated the food, Nike donated the shoes, and Kevin's agent donated the T-shirts, which had a gold triangle with Everett's No. 85 in the middle of it, along with a football and the camp's name.

"Port Arthur is a very poor area and the kids can't afford to attend a camp like the kids in the suburbs," Armstead said.

More than 100 youngsters attended the camp. Armstead said there was talk about charging a fee for future camps, with proceeds going to build parks and playgrounds in Port Arthur and to aid sickle-cell anemia patients in the area.

Kevin's injury may alter the foundation's future mission. Plans are in the works to have his foundation benefit those with spinal-cord injuries.

Kevin's generosity doesn't surprise Wiande. It's one of the things that attracted her to him. That and his unique personality. A lot of people refer to Kevin as being quiet, but those close to him know he has another side.

"Just because he's not the average 'hi-how-are-you-doing-guy?' people think he's not outgoing, but he really is," Wiande said. "Once you sit and get to know him, you realize how good a person he is. And he's very thoughtful. First and foremost, I found that the thing that really impressed me about him was how thoughtful he is with his family. He's very much a family person— and I am as well—and that's one of the main things that attracted us together. We're both family-oriented. And I just found it very special that he bought his mom a house and brought his little sisters here (to Humble, Texas) from Port Arthur. He's just very giving. When he needs something, he'll wait and do something for his sisters and his mom or me before he thinks of himself."

That characteristic, she said, "is what makes a person truly an inspiration, and others can see that good in him and it carries into them—and that's helped me grow as a person."

In the week before Christmas, Wiande was still driving Kevin to his therapy sessions and on his errands. Kevin looked forward to driving again, but he didn't want to rush things.

"I don't have control in my arms to react fast enough," he said. "My reaction time is not there yet."

He was working hard with his therapists, trying to improve the ability of his arms, hands, and legs.

"His hands still cramp up and are limited with dexterity," said Rafferty Laredo, Kevin's occupational therapist. "And although his upper extremities are functional, they still aren't 'normal.' The same is true with advanced skills with his legs to include high-level balance, running and advanced footwork."

Would those parts of the body ever get there, ever return to being normal?

That was the hope.

In the moments after Kevin suffered his injury, he lay motionless on the artificial turf at Ralph Wilson Stadium (top). A trainer held Kevin's head steady as he was treated on the field (middle), and teammates huddled in prayer (bottom).

Orthopedic surgeon Dr. Andrew Cappuccino described Kevin's injury as "catastrophic" and "life threatening" at a news conference on the day after the injury.

OUR THOUGHTS AND PRAYERS ARE WITH YOU KEVIN #85 *LOVE,* *Kiss* 98.5

Well-wishers placed a sign and flowers on the lawn outside Millard Fillmore Gates hospital, where Kevin was treated following his injury.

Kevin's teammates on the Buffalo Bills—including kicker Rian Lindell (left) and punter Brian Moorman—wore specially made warmup T-shirts in Kevin's honor before the game against Pittsburgh September 16, one week after Kevin's injury.

Dr. Teodoro Castillo, co-director of the Spinal Cord Injury program at Memorial Hermann-TIRR in Houston, discusses Kevin's recovery.

It was occupational therapist Rafferty Laredo's (standing) job to both strengthen Kevin's arms and legs and determine his limbs' potential for recovery.

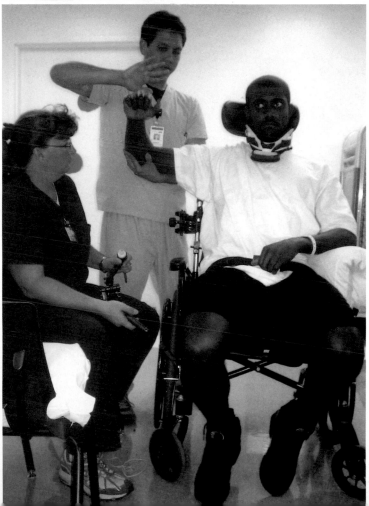

Kevin's rehabilitation program included pool sessions with physical therapist Darryn Atkinson to strengthen his upper body.

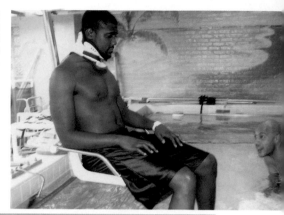

Kevin with Wiande Moore—his fiancé, best friend, and a constant source of support during the recovery from his spinal-cord injury. Wiande took a leave of absence from her job as a high school English teacher following Kevin's injury.

A shoulder-strengthening exercise doubles as decorating for Christmas as Kevin, working with occupational therapist Liza Criswell, reaches to hang colored clothespins from garland strung from the ceiling.

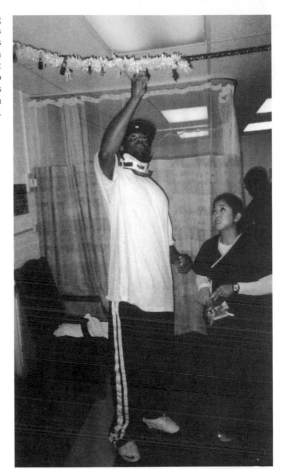

Kevin's three sisters, at the hospital to lend their love and support: From left to right: Kelli, 14; Herchell, 15; and Davia, 11, who faced her own medical crisis just one month before Kevin's injury when she fell into a diabetic coma.

Three people who were very important to Kevin's recovery: In the foreground, Dr. Teodoro "Ted" Castillo (left); physical therapist Darryn Atkinson; and in the background, fellow patient Virgil Calhoun, with whom Kevin developed a particularly close bond.

Kevin works carefully under the watchful eyes of occupational therapist Rafferty Laredo to build up his hand strength and small motor skills.

Kevin's presence never left the Bills during the 2007 season. (Clockwise from top left) He addressed the crowd and a national television audience during the November 18 game against New England. Then fans cheered and welcomed him back when he made his return to the stadium on December 23. He walked into the Bills locker room for an emotional meeting with his teammates before their game with the Giants.

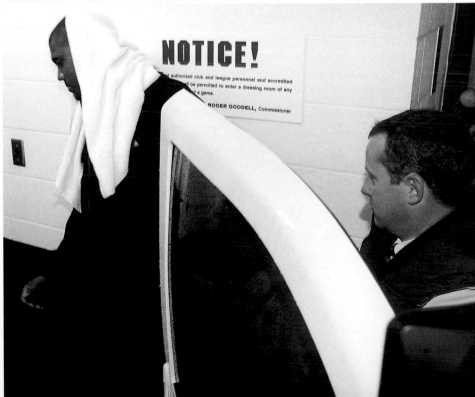

Only three months removed from his devastating spinal-cord injury suffered on a football field in Buffalo, Kevin Everett confidently strides into the future—thanks to the love and support provided by family and friends and to the top-notch medical care he received.

Kevin and his fiancée, Wiande Moore. The couple has set a Fall 2009 wedding date.

CHAPTER 10

THE LONG ROAD BACK

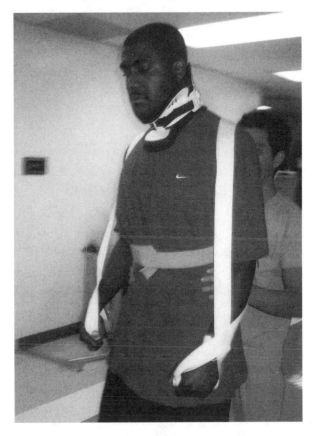

"The main thing that determines whether a person will start to make

a recovery after a spinal injury is the effect

of the trauma on the spine itself, and you can't do anything

to reverse that because it's already happened.

It also depends on how carefully the individual was rescued

and removed from the site and brought to the hospital."

Less than four months earlier, Kevin Everett was doing drills that would help him outmuscle a 250-pound linebacker.

Now, as he sat on a high-back oak chair in a room connected to the TIRR gym, he was undergoing an exercise in which, with his eyes closed, he tried to distinguish between six items: a piece of cotton, a key, a penny, a paper clip, a button, and a piece of sandpaper.

"Keep your eyes closed," said Rafferty Laredo, Kevin's affable occupational therapist.

It was late December, and Laredo took turns placing one of the items in Kevin's hand. Kevin rolled the item in his hand, round and round, until he felt he could identify it.

"It's a cotton ball; it's fuzzy," he said.

He was correct, and the therapist gave him another item.

"A key. I can feel the groves," Kevin said.

Again, he was correct, but he struggled with the next item, taking a long time as he rubbed a small piece of sandpaper that Laredo had placed in his hand.

"I can't really feel much of anything; it's real light," Kevin said.

Laredo wouldn't give him any clues.

"It's a paper clip," Kevin incorrectly decided.

The drill was designed to get sensation back in the hand and to see how much feedback was being sent to the brain.

Next, Laredo, using a safety pin, went through an exercise to see if Kevin could distinguish between sharp and dull. He gently rubbed different parts of the pin—sometimes the sharp side, sometimes the closed side—on Kevin's forearm and wrist.

Kevin, his eyes closed, was correct on five of the six times that he had to identify whether he was being touched by the sharp or the dull end of the pin. Then Laredo barely touched Kevin's pinky with the sharp end. Kevin, who still had numbness in some of his fingers, nearly jumped out of his chair.

"Ahhhhhhh!" he yelled.

With spinal-cord patients, different parts of the body are extra sensitive to certain touches and to hot and cold, said Laredo, explaining Kevin's surprising reaction.

Two days after that exercise, Kevin, wearing a Houston Astros baseball cap, went into a room adjacent to the gym and worked on a drill with Liza Criswell, another occupational therapist. She asked Kevin to attach colored clothespins to a piece of garland that was strung across the room. This was an activity to engage the shoulder, activate his reach, and improve his strength and coordination.

Kevin rolled the item in his hand, round and round, until he felt he could identify it.

Kevin did well. It takes him much longer than the average person—some of his motor skills are still trying to return—but he covered about 30 feet of the garland, from one side of the room to the other, with the clothespins.

He smiled softly, proud of the accomplishment.

"Okay, Kevin. Now can you take it down?" Criswell asked.

"Take it down? It looks nice up there," Kevin playfully protested.

"What?"

"It's a Christmas decoration," he explained.

His charm and good nature oozed. Criswell surrendered. The clothespins stayed attached.

"Okay, we'll leave them up there for a while," she said.

Advantage, Everett.

❖ ❖ ❖

In the gym at TIRR, near the world map that has pushpins showing about 40 countries from where patients have traveled to be treated there—Saudi Arabia, Poland, Venezuela, Germany,

India, Costa Rica, Kuwait, and Ecuador are among them—Laredo is helping Kevin perform exercises and drills to regain as much motion and strength as possible.

Now the therapist's goal is to get Kevin's arms to work as normally as possible.

"He can't manipulate some objects and can't control with force," Laredo said.

Kevin won't be able to throw a 90-mph fastball anytime soon.

"Not yet, anyway," Laredo said.

The occupational therapist is also fine-tuning the way Kevin can work his hands. He can open and close them, "but the motor control and manipulation is not there," said Laredo, still trying to help Kevin regain sensation in his hands.

"Anytime I see a guy laying on the field and guys kneeling around him, it brings me back to my injury."

Regaining sensation was important so that Kevin could avoid injuries. The previous week, he had cut the middle finger of his right hand and, because of nerve damage from the spinal injury, he didn't have sensation in it. He didn't realize he had been injured until he saw blood.

"Either you compensate for (losing) the sensation or figure out a way for it to return," said Laredo, who was working on the latter. "It's important for me to find a way to get it back. I still haven't figured out what to do about it."

Kevin worked on an exercise to improve his finger dexterity and his hand-eye coordination. "He doesn't have sensation in his fingers, so he's using his eyes to compensate," Laredo said.

As he goes through his rehab, Kevin has a role model in New Jersey, Adam Taliaferro, who went through a similar ordeal when he was paralyzed while making a tackle for Penn State in 2000. There are other parallels between the two men. Both were 25 years old at the time of Kevin's injury. Both were highly touted in high school. And both figured to one day make an impact in the pros.

During breaks in his rehab, Kevin read *Miracle in the Making: The Adam Taliaferro Story*, a book Taliaferro had sent to him with this inscription: "It's great to see your amazing recovery. Stay strong and continue the great progress. Your recovery has been an inspiration to me! God bless—Adam Taliaferro, #43"

Taliaferro, who is more than seven years removed from his injury, is in his final semester of law school at Rutgers-Camden and has already been hired by a Philadelphia law firm, upon graduation. When he was injured, Taliaferro defied the odds. Three different doctors told his parents to make their home wheelchair accessible; they explained that Taliaferro, who was then a Penn State freshman, would likely never walk.

A little more than three months later, Taliaferro, with the help of metal crutches, walked out of Magee Rehabilitation Hospital in Philadelphia. He now walks with a limp and his right hand doesn't open all the way—nerve damage from his paralyzing tackle against Ohio State—but other than that, his life is normal.

Taliaferro was watching the Philadelphia Eagles-Green Bay Packers opener on September 9 when the TV network cut into that game and showed a clip of Everett's paralyzing tackle.

"Even with me getting paralyzed, you never expect it to happen to anyone else," Taliaferro said. "You expect him to be able to get up and walk again. They showed all the guys praying all around him, and anytime I see a guy laying on the field and guys kneeling around him, it brings me back to my injury."

As Taliaferro watched the video clip of Kevin, he copied the Bills and Broncos players—he started praying.

During Kevin's rehabilitation, Taliaferro constantly scoured the Internet for updates on his condition. He could relate to the grueling rehab, one that Kevin often downplays.

"It's like (football) practice, but it's different because your body is so weak and the rehab drains everything out of you on a daily basis," Taliaferro said. "You feel both mentally and physically drained. I remember going back to my room and feeling just mentally tired. It was one of the most draining things I've ever gone through and I'm just thankful I had a strong support system to get through it."

Taliaferro was referring to his mother, father, and brother, along with relatives, friends, teammates, coaches, and Penn State's support staff.

"One person cannot get through it alone," he said. "You need help."

"Every game I watch, I see someone I played against, and you can't help but wish you were out there, too."

Likewise, Kevin's support system, headed by Wiande, Patricia, and his three sisters, has played a major role in his recovery. Taliaferro cautioned Kevin to stay persistent in the next phase of his recovery.

"When you get some recovery back, there are always things that have to be fine-tuned," Taliaferro said. "I got back on my feet, but it wasn't done. There are a lot of things, even to this day, that I have to work on—cardio, strengthening my hands, and so many other things. I have to be cognizant that, even today, it's a struggle to maintain what I regained."

Taliaferro works out lightly at a gym daily, but he is still unable to run—seven years after breaking his neck. It takes him longer to do things, such as eating and getting dressed. But he has adjusted.

He doesn't have good use of his right hand, so he has learned to feed himself with his left hand. He had problems writing notes in law school—initially, someone did the task for him—but he is now able to type them into his computer.

"Thankfully, I can do almost everything," he said.

Expect Kevin to go through some emotional pain when he watches his NFL teammates play on TV, Taliaferro said. He speaks from experience. Several of his Penn State teammates—guys like Kansas City Chiefs running back Larry Johnson, Chicago Bears nose tackle Anthony Adams, Buffalo Bills safety Bryan Scott, Arizona Cardinals wide receiver Bryant Johnson, and Detroit Lions tight end Sean McHugh—are thriving in the NFL. Bills cornerback Jabari Greer, whom Taliaferro met when they were on a recruiting visit to the University of Tennessee, is another NFL player with ties to the law student. The same goes for Dallas Cowboys cornerback Nathan Jones, who was in the same defensive backfield with Taliaferro in a high school all-star game.

Taliaferro watches these players on TV and wonders how his career would have turned out if it wasn't for his life-changing injury.

"I didn't come to grips with it until the first Penn State practice I went to after the injury," he said. At the time, he was helping coach the defensive backs. "And then I realized it was over."

Taliaferro watches NFL games now and, for a few fleeting seconds, wonders what could have been.

"You're always wondering. It's a question I never had answered," he said. "Every game I watch, I see someone I played against, and you can't help but wish you were out there, too."

When those thoughts enter his mind, he refocuses and thinks back to Magee Rehabilitation Hospital in Philadelphia—just as Kevin will always have TIRR in his memory—and he quickly loses the sadness he feels for not being able to play football.

"For me, whenever I think of those thoughts, I think that's a selfish thought," Taliaferro said. "I think of the people who are (moving) around Magee in wheelchairs...people who can't walk. I got on with my life. I'm walking, and for me to be moping around or feeling bad about not playing, that's just selfish, so I get it out of my mind."

The hypothermia treatment, a cooling method that some think contributed to Kevin's recovery, wasn't available when Taliaferro was injured. But he hopes injuries like his and Everett's will raise awareness and spark research for spinal-cord injuries. "I had perfect care and I'm just so blessed with the team of doctors I had at Ohio State and Penn State," he said. "I'm sure Kevin feels the same way about his care."

Treating spinal injuries and educating the public on how to prevent them are two goals of the Adam Taliaferro Foundation, a New Jersey-based nonprofit organization that assists injured athletes. Thus far, the foundation—started by Taliaferro's high school football coach Larry Ginsburg when it looked like Taliaferro would be confined to a wheelchair and that his home needed to become handicap-accessible—has raised more than $200,000 for injured athletes.

"Something good came out of it," Taliaferro said of his injury.

Everett hopes to start a similar foundation.

"I tell people the injury was the bad part, but everything else has been good," said Taliaferro, who, in addition to going to law school and assisting with his foundation, has become a part-time football broadcaster in the Philadelphia region. "We've been able to help so many people with the foundation—not only the injured athletes but the families who are dealing with it. There are things I'm doing now that I could never have done if I didn't get hurt, and I'm meeting people I never would have met."

Taliaferro turned a catastrophic situation into a positive.

Kevin Everett is anxious to do the same.

❖❖❖

After returning from Buffalo where he was joyfully reunited with his teammates, Kevin spent time with his family in the Humble, Texas, home he had purchased for them the previous year. An impressive 35-foot foyer, covered with Italian ceramic tile, greets visitors as they enter the two-story suburban home. So do the words that are framed and sitting on a table in the cozy family room.

The words are particularly poignant to Patricia this Christmas:

"Nothing you will ever own, no worldly thing you will ever acquire, will be worth so much as the love of your children."

The room is comfortable, with two oversized brown leather couches, a fireplace with six stockings hanging from it, and a wall-mounted TV. Adjacent to the family room is an open-air kitchen with granite counter tops and top-of-the-line appliances. Around the corner is a tiny room that comes alive because of the beautifully decorated Christmas tree. In a few days, the room will be filled with presents, just like any Christmas.

But this was far from a typical Christmas.

Kevin and his family spent Christmas with relatives in Port Arthur—a 75-minute drive from their home in Humble—while Wiande stayed with her family in Spring. They would have plenty of Christmases together in the near future. This was a year to cherish the time with their families.

Kevin, his mom, and his three sisters visited with Jackie Adams, who is Patricia's sister and Kevin's aunt, and other family members. "It was a nice, simple Christmas," Patricia said.

She paused.

"It was a very blessed Christmas for me because I had all my children there—after almost losing two of them," she said.

Patricia was referring to Kevin's catastrophic September injury, and the fact that 11-year-old Davia was in a diabetic coma the month before that.

The family members munched on barbecued chicken, ribs, and sausage and talked about all their good times together...and all the good times to come.

"It was a great Christmas, and not solely for my recovery," Kevin said. "To tell you the truth, every day is great for me. Every day is Christmas."

Patricia excitedly talked about the post-Christmas gift her son had planned for her—a trip to Las Vegas. But that was in the future. As she digested her holiday meal, she smiled and glanced lovingly at Kevin and Davia. She smiled and thought that the trip to Vegas was secondary to the gifts she had sitting at her table.

"I told him that maybe the reason for this happening is an opportunity to stop and sort of reevaluate your life and where you are."

❖ ❖ ❖

Kevin's injury, Wiande said, has made her treat each day as if it's special.

"People constantly use phrases like, 'Don't take life for granted' or 'Live every day like it's your last one,'" she said. "But when I first came here (the Houston hospital), I finally realized that you can't take life for granted." People who complain that they have to get up for work in the morning "need to thank God you have legs to get up and walk—or that you actually woke up in the morning. That's a blessing in itself."

Ever since she was a shy little girl who pretended she was a teacher by instructing a group of her stuffed animals, Wiande had been a loving person. Being around TIRR had made her even more compassionate.

"You come to the hospital and you see people who can't even

get out of their wheelchair," she said, "and the only thing they want is to get up and walk."

One particular patient particularly inspired her.

"He was a police officer and he could move his upper body but not his lower body," she said. "And when I saw him, he was telling his story; he got in a car accident and I was like, Oh my goodness, that's something that a lot of people don't think about because you have legs and you have a 'this-isn't-going-to-happen-to-me' (attitude) until it does. And when it happened to Kevin, to somebody I love, it actually really opened my eyes—God opened my eyes—that life is really precious and you need to take every day as if it's your last.... And don't just say it."

"It was a very blessed Christmas for me because I had all my children there—after almost losing two of them."

Rafferty Laredo, TIRR's occupational therapist, has had many heartfelt conversations with Kevin about his injury.

"I told him that maybe the reason for this happening is an opportunity to stop and sort of reevaluate your life and where you are," he said.

Laredo senses that Kevin is a happy, grounded person.

"Maybe he's much closer to Wiande now, or maybe he's made some new friends, or maybe he has touched the lives of people around him in the gym who were inspired by him," Laredo said. "But he'll also tell you that he was absolutely inspired by all the people who are around him, so I think that's a beautiful thing to be able to say there's a reason for this happening—and I'm not limiting it to just his ability to walk again or limiting it to the ability to move his arms, but to be able to say, 'Where am I in life?' and that it's good."

❖❖❖

Barbara Jackson, the case manager at TIRR, continued to send medical reports to the Bills' trainer. News of Kevin's accomplishments quickly spread around Buffalo. Every day, it seemed, Kevin would get more sensation in a part of his body that had lost it. The accomplishments were gradual but steady. They were also uplifting.

"It would be easy to look back on it now and say I expected him to be where he is, but I didn't really know what to expect," Darryn Atkinson said in late December.

Kevin's road to recovery started because of perfect execution by the medical team on the field at Ralph Wilson Stadium.

"Before he got here, we didn't know how strong he really was," added Atkinson, the physical therapist. "Once we saw him and got to evaluate him, it was pretty clear that his legs were pretty strong and there was a lot more arm and shoulder weakness, so at that point, we were confident that, unless something happened we weren't aware of, he would be able to get up and start walking eventually. But I didn't really expect him to get to that point quite as quickly as he did.

"We didn't expect it, but it's something we were definitely shooting for. I mean, we really had the opportunity to get there."

The patient who couldn't lift a spoon during his early days at TIRR was regaining his strength.

"I curled 50 pounds the other day," Kevin told a visitor.

The visitor looked up from his glasses and his eyebrows arched in amazement.

"Fifty pounds?!"

Kevin laughed heartily.

"You should have seen your expression," he said.

Curling 50 pounds would be admirable for a healthy person.

"I couldn't do that," Kevin confessed, "unless I wanted to get facial reconstruction."

The Kevin who arrived at TIRR on September 21 wouldn't have been so playful. But it was late December, and so what if he could only curl about 20 pounds? There were Christmas decorations hanging all around TIRR, and Kevin Everett was in a holiday mood.

In truth, he seemed to be in that kind of mood every day.

❖ ❖ ❖

Laredo, who has been working at TIRR since 2000, said Kevin's progress was "at the top" among patients he has treated.

"I would say he's at the top because he's extremely functional," Laredo said. "Typically, with central-cord (patients), you would expect some level of lower-extremity return, pretty decent lower-extremity return, but not often do you see good functional ability of the upper extremities, which involve shoulders and the arms and the ability to use your hands."

Dr. William Donovan, medical director of the Houston hospital, said Kevin's road to recovery started because of perfect execution by the medical team on the field at Ralph Wilson Stadium.

"The main thing that determines whether a person will start to make a recovery after a spinal injury is the effect of the trauma on the spine itself," Donovan said, "and you can't do anything to reverse that because it's already happened. It also depends on how carefully the individual was rescued and removed from the site and brought to the hospital. If it is done very carefully, then we can avoid any secondary injury, beyond what the event itself caused."

Teodoro Castillo, Kevin's attending physician at TIRR, recalled treating a woman who fell down the steps and broke her neck.

Her father, in a state of panic, picked her up and took her to the hospital.

"And that," Castillo said, "made her worse."

The patient should not have been moved since her neck needed to be immobilized. If the head is jerked or flexed, it can severely compound the effects of the original trauma and contribute to paralysis.

When a spinal-cord injury occurs, a quick and careful removal from the site is imperative. So is making sure the person has adequate oxygenation and maintenance of blood pressure, "so we can deliver the oxygen to the tissue," Donovan said.

In Kevin's case, this was all carried out. In textbook fashion.

Donovan said the "original insult" or injury "is the main determining fact" in how much recovery the patient can expect.

Educating the public on treating neck injuries is critical, Donovan said. According to the National Spinal Cord Injury Statistical Center, the annual incidence of spinal-cord injuries—not including those who die at the scene of an accident—is approximately 40 cases per one million people in the United States. That translates to about 11,000 new cases each year.

"I'm still in a wheelchair and he walked out of the hospital."

The statistical center noted that those figures are based on the last spinal-cord incidence study in the United States, which was compiled in the 1970s.

As of 2006, it was estimated that 253,000 people in the United States are living with spinal-cord injuries.

"The important thing to remember is that after a spinal-cord injury, the spinal cord really shuts down, whether it's a minor or major injury," Donovan said. "The only way we really know whether it was minor or major is after time goes by. If within the first 24, 48 hours recovery starts to occur, then we look back and say it was probably a minor injury, but if we go out three months and nothing has come back and the person has no function at all, then we look back and say it was a major injury. But nobody knows when he's lying there on the football field, so therefore you have to assume the injury is incomplete and take all the precautions that you can during the rescue process."

Marc Buoniconti knows all about complete spinal-cord injuries. Buoniconti, the son of Nick Buoniconti, the Hall of Fame linebacker who starred with the Miami Dolphins, was paralyzed while making a tackle for The Citadel in a 1985 game at East Tennessee State.

The injury was the same as Kevin's, a dislocation of the C3/C4 vertebrae. Yet, more than 22 years later, Buoniconti still sits in a wheelchair.

"You don't know if it's a complete injury until you find out if you can move something," said Marc Buoniconti, who serves as president of the Buoniconti Fund to Cure Paralysis and as ambassador for the Miami Project to Cure Paralysis. "Who knows if Kevin would have been incomplete if he didn't get all the care he got. If I had the same medical care and treatment, mine may have been incomplete. The difference between my injury and Kevin's is nothing. It was the same injury. But the outcome is *everything* because of the care he received.

"I'm still in a wheelchair and he walked out of the hospital."

Buoniconti believes hypothermia played a major role in Everett's recovery and said he was "ecstatic for Kevin and for the field of spinal-cord injuries."

Kevin's recovery was part of the remarkable teamwork he shared with the medical teams in Buffalo and then in Houston, Donovan said. The treatment he received on the field, in the ambulance, and in the hospital in Buffalo was as close to perfect as possible. The same could be said for his treatment at TIRR, the rehab hospital in Houston.

Teamwork, Donovan said, "is the essence of rehabilitation. The patient is part of a team, and that team brings all of its expertise together, led by the physician, who's captain of the team." With spinal injuries, "it's different from other branches of medicine. It's not just the doctor and the patient, or the doctor and the nurse and the patient. Here, if you want to do it right, you have to have contributions from the various different specialists and all pulling in the same direction."

In other words, Team Kevin.

❖ ❖ ❖

Dr. Castillo, a shy but warm man whom Donovan calls "Teddy," was captain of Team Kevin. Still, he downplayed his role in the recovery. He said the most important factor that worked in Kevin's favor may have been the extremely quick time it took for doctors to evaluate the situation and begin operating on Kevin.

Kevin was injured on September 9 at about 2:35 PM. Thirteen minutes later, he was lifted into an ambulance and, within minutes, was given two IV lines of iced saline. At 3:20 PM, he was at Millard Fillmore Gates Hospital in downtown Buffalo, where he quickly had X-rays, a CT scan, and magnetic resonance imaging (MRI). Usually, injured players are taken to Buffalo General, which is about a mile closer. But Dr. Andrew Cappuccino, the Bills' orthopedist, had instructed the ambulance driver to go to Millard Fillmore Gates Hospital because he knew it had MRI technicians available 24 hours a day. He knew this by happenstance—two days earlier he went to the hospital to be with an injured football player who was his son's high school teammate. While he was there, he learned about the MRI technicians' availability and filed it in his mind.

At most hospitals, "you have to call in a technician, and they have to warm up the machine and it could take hours before it's done," Cappuccino said. "I knew they had a technician there."

For Kevin, the rapidity of the tests meant his surgery could be performed sooner—and that was one of the many factors that worked to his advantage.

"When I saw him in the surgery holding area, it was around 5:00 PM," said Dr. Kevin Gibbons, who worked with Cappuccino on Kevin's surgery.

A few tests were done in the holding area, and Kevin was brought into the operating room at 5:40 PM, Gibbons said. After some more X-rays, Gibbons said, the first incision was made at 6:30 PM, a little less than four hours after the injury occurred.

Kevin's injury-to-surgery time frame was quicker than the average spinal-cord patient's. Much quicker.

"The average guy who crashes his car into a tree sits there for one or two hours before someone finds him, then he's cut from the vehicle and studies are done and he's put in traction," Cappuccino said. "It might take 10...12 hours" for surgery to be performed.

In Kevin's case, "we had a working diagnosis on the field and made appropriate calls, and they cleared the trauma room at the hospital as quickly as it could have been done," Cappuccino added. "And all this while we were cooling him down."

While there is a disagreement among the medical community as to what keyed Kevin's recovery, everyone seems to agree that the presurgery events could not have gone any smoother.

"With any bone or disc encroaching on the spinal cord, you have to relieve that pressure as soon as you can do it," Castillo said. "Now if I got injured in a car wreck, would I be in the operating room (that quickly)? What do you think? Probably not, because it takes a while, so that could be something that probably made him better."

The quickness in which the surgery was performed, Castillo hinted, was probably more important than the moderate hypothermia, which was administered before and after the operation.

"When you get an injury like this, everyone should know that time is of the essence," Castillo said. "Time and stability."

And faith, Kevin said.

If he was delivering a message to spinal-cord patients, Kevin said, he would tell them, "Believe in God. Believe and really just put your heart into God, because no one else can bring you that peace, whatever the situation. Just remember God gave you that peace. He's somebody that you need."

❖ ❖ ❖

Kevin approached his rehab with the same intensity he displayed at Bills practice sessions. Among teammates' discussions about Kevin, a common theme emerged: No one will outwork him.

That made Team Kevin's job much easier, especially after a feeling-out period ended and both sides felt comfortable with each other.

Castillo called it "a pleasure to work with him, as well as Wiande and his mom. I was in contact with all three of them when he was here as an inpatient.... Kevin's a quiet guy, like I am, and he doesn't like a lot of media and I respect him for that, because it's really hard to adjust to this injury...(especially) if you're a high-profile person like him. We've seen significant improvement since the day he came, and I know people will say it's the doctors, the therapists, and TIRR, but it all boils down really to Kevin. All we did really was tell Kevin what to do and all the work really is Kevin and the support he's getting from his family, so I give him the compliment for the motivation, the energy, and the focus. And Wiande for the support."

"Wiande has definitely played a significant role," said Laredo, the TIRR occupational therapist. "When you talk to Kevin about his recovery…he attributes a lot of his success to the support system he's had around him and knowing that people around him love him and actually care about him very much."

Between rehab exercises, Kevin would mingle with the patients and medical staff or grab something to eat in the hospital cafeteria. Sometimes, he and Wiande would play games—checkers, cards, *Scrabble, Guess Who?*, and others—to help Kevin improve his hand dexterity and coordination.

"When you get an injury like this, everyone should know that time is of the essence."

There was another reason: They liked beating the pants off each other.

"We're both competitive," said Wiande, the one-time elite track star at Miami.

"*She's* the one who's competitive," Kevin disagreed. "It gets intense for her. It's not intense for me because it's easy" to beat her.

Wiande shook her head and smiled. She let Kevin's comment pass without a rebuttal.

The support provided by Wiande and Patricia, Castillo said, is what put Kevin in the right frame of mind to cope with the situation and focus on his recovery.

"I didn't have to call a psychologist for him because, for one, he actually said, 'I think I'm okay,'" Castillo said. "All the patients who come in here with this type of injury, I believe, will have some degree of what I call reactive depression—you know, you can't do what you used to do," and it affects the mental aspect of the recovery.

"But his family has been there for him, and Wiande has been

there for him, and his mom is also great. I've spent time with her and she really is a trooper, too."

Patricia Dugas told Castillo that he and his staff should keep pushing Kevin.

"She would say, 'Just let me know if Kevin slows down and I'll be there telling him (to keep going),'" Castillo recalled. "But we knew it wasn't going to be a problem because, as I said, Kevin is really focused and knows what he's going for."

Kevin showed no signs of depression, Castillo said. He was withdrawn for a while but never at the point where it affected his rehab. "Based on his therapy progress here, he never really showed signs that some patients have like, 'Oh, I don't want to do therapy.' He's always been focused," Castillo said. "So the team didn't see any signs that he's kind of depressed in terms of affecting his routine."

"Coach never exploited it and used it for a rallying cry, but he respected Kevin and that came through."

Kevin's teammates also put him in a good frame of mind. They filmed messages from the Bills' lounge every Tuesday.

The upbeat videos were then sent to Kevin.

"You're doing great," tight end Robert Royal said in one of them. "Keep pushing."

"I love you," cornerback Jabari Greer said in another.

"We're playing for you," safety Bryan Scott told him. "Hang in there; we're thinking of you."

All of Buffalo—the city, the team, the fans—seemed to rally around No. 85.

"I couldn't be more thrilled for the way things turned out for Kevin," said Paul Lancaster, the Bills' executive. "It's amazing to be part of an organization where everyone steps up. The organization put people in position to help in any way they could, and that meant so much to the family."

Bills president Ralph Wilson instructed Lancaster to do whatever he needed to do to assist Kevin and his family. He did. Lancaster was by the family's side during the traumatic days in September, and he made two trips to Houston to be with Kevin and Wiande at TIRR.

"Everyone in the organization did a great job of coming together," Lancaster said, mentioning head coach Jauron, Scott Berchtold, the team's vice president of communications, and Jim Overdorf, the Bills' vice president of football administration, among others.

"The players, the wives, they all were in this together," he said.

Lancaster singled out the compassionate Jauron, Buffalo's veteran coach, for the way he handled the situation.

"He gave Kevin his utmost respect," Lancaster said. "Coach never exploited it and used it for a rallying cry, but he respected Kevin and that came through."

THE ROLE OF HYPOTHERMIA

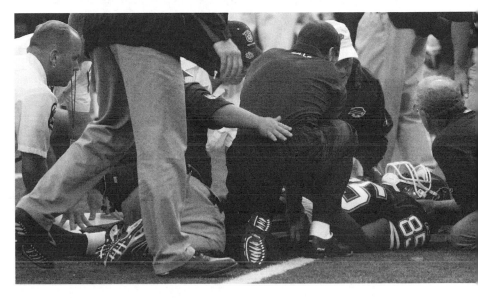

CHAPTER 11

"I wish I was in the same boat as Kevin Everett right now.

Dr. Cappuccino had a lot of guts

to do it. Maybe some of his colleagues are saying

otherwise...but from what I understand,

any decrease in temperature is helpful."

Kevin Everett's remarkable recovery begs a question: How much of a role—if any—can be attributed to the relatively new use of hypothermia, the cooling treatment that lowers a body's temperature?

The medical community is divided.

In fact, the two doctors who performed Kevin's spinal surgery—Andrew Cappuccino and Kevin Gibbons—have somewhat differing opinions on the treatment's effect.

Hypothermia slows the patient's metabolism, allowing cells to survive longer when deprived of oxygen. Cappuccino explained that animal tests have demonstrated that cooling limits the swelling and the toxic chemical release that follow a spinal-cord injury.

"People are always skeptical when there's something new."

Cappuccino said he was "convinced" that hypothermia was a factor in Kevin's recovery. It was the first time he had used hypothermia on a patient and the first time he knew of it being used on any professional athlete.

"Hypothermia wasn't the absolute (factor), but one of many factors" that contributed, Cappuccino said. "It was the perfect storm for treating a spinal-cord injury—the immediate attention on the field...the utilization of hypothermia and steroids, the spine being realigned."

If another case arose similar to Kevin's, Cappuccino said, he would use hypothermia.

"Kevin's cord was not cut, and, yes, I would do it again on any patient like that," he said. "Despite the controversy and some doubters out there, I do know what works."

Some doctors, he said, don't like to use "something completely different in the management of a spinal-cord injury. People are always skeptical when there's something new." In the 1800s, "when (Louis) Pasteur said sterile technique was important to surgery for preventing infections, he was laughed out of the business, but he was right."

Gibbons said hypothermia may have contributed to Kevin's recovery, but that it was probably less important than other factors.

In the December 17 *Sports Illustrated* article, it was reported that on September 10—the day after Everett's injury—his body was placed on hypothermia in the predawn hours and, within two hours, had cooled to 91.5 degrees. That morning, the story said, Kevin was able to squeeze his thighs against Cappuccino's hands.

Gibbons said some of those facts are inaccurate—and that he didn't want to give "false hope" to people who think hypothermia is *the* solution to curing paralysis.

When a patient is trying to recover from paralysis, the first movement is the most important development—that is, if the movement is ever made, Gibbons said. "When you move a little, chances of moving (a lot) are pretty good," he added. "The real leap is when you start moving."

When Kevin showed his first movement after the surgery, it was 5:00 AM on September 10 and his temperature was around 98.6 degrees, said Gibbons, emphasizing he was not in a hypothermic state at that time, as the *Sports Illustrated* article implied. (His temperature, in fact, was about seven degrees warmer than the magazine implied.)

Kevin's movement "was before we started effective cooling," Gibbons said. "The fact that he subsequently recovered so fast was helped by hypothermia, but it was not *the* thing in this patient."

Gibbons said it was important to understand Kevin's temperature at different times in the process.

The iced saline was administered in the ambulance, and Kevin's temperature was "98-something" when he arrived at Millard Fillmore Gates Hospital, Gibbons said. "So he really wasn't iced, and he didn't get very cool during surgery. He was around 96 during surgery. He didn't get what we'd call out of the ordinary."

Following the surgery, which ended at 9:35 PM on September 9, medical personnel tried to keep Kevin's temperature down with what they call "surface cooling." Cooling blankets were used in the process.

"He had a CT scan done and for most of the night, his temperature was in the normal range—around 98," Gibbons said.

Gibbons said the medical staff was hoping to get Kevin's temperature down to around 93.

"Moderate hypothermia is in the 92 to 94 range, but we never got there—even with the surface cooling," he said.

When Dr. Cappuccino examined Kevin at 5:00 AM, he could "move his legs a little," Gibbons said, adding that his temperature at the time was around 98.6. "And between 6:00 and 6:30 AM, he could move his legs even more, and his temperature was at 98.4."

"What has hit the press is crazy. We want to raise hope but not false hope."

Gibbons said he didn't think the hypothermia was needed when he examined Kevin at 6:30 AM, but that he changed his mind when Kevin's temperature began rising a few minutes later. That's when he and Cappuccino were in agreement.

At 6:35 AM, Gibbons said, Kevin's temperature started to climb; it was at 99 degrees, and it was clear that the surface cooling "was not working."

It was time to prepare to start hypothermia. This treatment would be performed with a machine attached to a special catheter placed inside a large vein. Cold fluid was circulated in and out of the catheter, cooling the blood as it flowed by but not mixing the cold fluid with his blood.

Cappuccino had to call a hospital security guard to unlock a doctor's office, where the needed catheter had been placed.

At 8:30 AM, with Kevin's temperature between 99 and 100 degrees, he showed even more movement in an exam performed by Gibbons and Dr. Ken Snyder. "He was moving his hips, knees, and ankles," Gibbons said.

Gibbons acknowledged that "it took us a while to get the catheter put in; it was put in between 8:00 AM and 9:00 AM. By 10:30 AM, Kevin's temperature had dropped to 93, he said.

The media reports that said Kevin was cooled when he first moved his legs, Gibbons said, were inaccurate.

"It's a factual misstatement of cause and effect and is a critical error," he said. "It's like arguing that so-and-so is the best coach of all time because he won four Super Bowls, but then you find out he didn't win any Super Bowls."

Gibbons said he is hopeful that hypothermia played an important role in Kevin's recovery but that more studies have to be done before a determination can be made. He added that he didn't want to give "false hope" to people who think hypothermia can cure paralysis.

Gibbons said some of the media reports on hypothermia misrepresented the treatment's effectiveness.

"What has hit the press is crazy," he said, pointing out that he is a hypothermia researcher and is not against the treatment. "We want to raise hope but not false hope."

Added Gibbons, referring to the first hypothermia treatment that was done in the ambulance: "The idea that two liters of saline in someone's Playmate cooler would have made someone walk... is truly false hope."

❖ ❖ ❖

Dr. Barth Green, chairman of the department of neurological surgery at the University of Miami School of Medicine and cofounder of The Miami Project to Cure Paralysis, has been researching hypothermia since the 1960s. He has invested a lot of time and energy in the subject, so it's understandable that he was ecstatic with Kevin Everett's results.

As Kevin recovered, Green became a media darling. Several of his quotes bubbled with euphoria.

Dietrich came up with the idea of mildly cooling the patient.

Two days after Kevin's injury, Green publicly stated that Everett would "walk out of the hospital."

In one media account, Green called it "a spectacular example of what people can do. To me, it's like putting the first man on the moon or splitting the atom. We've shown that, if the right treatment is given to people who have a catastrophic injury, they could walk away from it."

In the *Boston Globe*'s September 23 edition—two weeks after Kevin sustained his injury—Green said, "He's out of the woods and on his way to walking soon. The best-case scenario is he'll walk and be very independent. He'll be able to work, but not as a football player, probably. The Miami Project has been swamped with calls from everywhere. You're going to see patients across the country getting this treatment next week because of what Dr. Cappuccino did. It will also work for car-accident victims and heart attacks. This is a very big deal."

Green became connected to Everett because of his friendship with Buffalo Bills president Ralph Wilson. Green performed surgery on Wilson about 15 years ago.

"We became dear friends," Green said.

Because of that friendship—and because of his expertise in the field—Green was an unofficial consultant in Kevin's case. He would occasionally discuss Kevin's condition with Cappuccino, the Bills' orthopedist.

In December 2006, Cappuccino had attended a national medical conference in West Palm Beach, Florida. The conference included a hypothermia lecture, given by W. Dalton Dietrich, science director of the Miami Project to Cure Paralysis.

Dietrich was connected to Green, who believes Everett's recovery demonstrates the Miami Project's progress. Over the years, Wilson, the Bills' president, has been one of the Miami Project's biggest donors. "He's donated millions," Green said, adding that there was "karma between me and the Miami Project and the Bills."

Green said he did hypothermia research in the 1960s and 1970s when he was a medical student. As a resident physician in the early '70s, he worked at Wesley Memorial Hospital, one of Northwestern University's affiliated facilities in Chicago.

"We actually cut open a spine and poured cold saline on it," he recalled, adding that the saline was at 39 degrees. "I was cooling spinal-cord patients experimentally. We found we could save function at the back of the cord, but couldn't effectively cool the front of the cord—the part that affects movement."

The experimental treatment worked partially, he said. "The patient recovered sensation, but not movement...and movement is mainly what we wanted, so we abandoned the project."

But, Green added, "we realized the potential."

In medical circles, hypothermia "was a hot topic in the '60s and '70s, and then it was sort of ignored in the '80s and '90s until Dr. Dietrich looked at a different type of hypothermia."

Dietrich came up with the idea of mildly cooling the patient, Green said. Until then, the experiments had been done by cooling patients at 39 degrees; in the new technique, they would be cooled to just 92 degrees.

"Dr. Dietrich did the research on animals and found we were able to protect the spinal cord more effectively" at 92 degrees, Green said.

Green said he first tried moderate hypothermia on a patient five years ago and that, since then, he has used it on "hundreds" who have had spinal-cord surgery for paralysis.

Most of those patients had already had dangerous surgeries on their spinal cords and were either paralyzed before their operations or were at a high risk of being paralyzed during surgery, he said.

Green estimated he has used hypothermia on 30 trauma patients in similar condition to Kevin Everett—and that 25 percent of those patients are now walking.

"But none were done as early as Kevin's hypothermia," he said.

Starting hypothermia about 15 minutes after an injury—as was done in Kevin's case—may be unprecedented.

"He opened up Pandora's box for us," Green said. Because of the early treatment, "we are suspicious it will help people, but don't have scientific proof yet. We think the key is using the hypothermia in minutes, not hours."

As a result of Kevin's success, Green has met with paramedics and informed them that the hypothermia should be used early in spinal-cord patients. "Because of Kevin, we're reorganizing our cooling program and will begin cooling patients in an ambulance in the future, instead of waiting until they get to the hospital," Green said.

Hypothermia risks include pneumonia (which Kevin developed), cardiac arrhythmia, and major infections.

"What would you rather have—pneumonia for a week and walk out of a hospital, or not be able to walk at all?" asked Marc

Buoniconti, a Miami Project ambassador who was paralyzed in a 1985 football game.

"Nothing is a no-risk (treatment)," Green said. "But treatment using hypothermia is FDA approved for heart attacks, so we're taking an approved treatment for one thing and using it for another, like what Dr. Cappuccino did."

Green downplayed the fact that, according to Gibbons, Kevin had a normal temperature and wasn't hypothermic when his legs first moved after surgery.

"We think the key is using the hypothermia in minutes, not hours."

"That doesn't minimize hypothermia; not at all," he said. "Even if the temperature is a half degree under normal, it's the start of hypothermia, and many trauma patients come in with a higher temperature...and high temperature is dangerous and destroys the nervous system."

Kevin's temperature was never allowed to get excessively high, he said.

Green acknowledged there is no way of knowing how much hypothermia aided the recovery.

"Only God knows what percentage it was," he said. "Was it 90 percent? Fifty percent? Twenty-eight percent? No one knows. A lot of colleagues pooh-poohed it and said he would have gotten better anyway. Dr. Cappuccino says that's not the case. Kevin had the same injury Marc Buoniconti had and (Marc's) in a wheelchair.

"Let's say Kevin would have been one of the lucky ones to recover (without hypothermia). It would have taken months, years. And Kevin was walking within weeks after his injury. There's no way the naysayers can say it didn't have a major component to his recovery."

Kevin took steps with a walker exactly one month after his

injury, a stunningly quick recovery.

Buoniconti, who was paralyzed making a tackle for The Citadel in 1985, is convinced that hypothermia is one of the main reasons Kevin is walking.

"I wish I would have had it," he said. "I wish I was in the same boat as Kevin Everett right now. Dr. Cappuccino had a lot of guts to do it. Maybe some of his colleagues are saying otherwise…but from what I understand, any decrease in temperature is helpful. One study says that people injured in the north were better off because of the cold environment as opposed to (spinal-cord) injuries in the south."

All of the doctors agree that more studies have to be made to find out how much quickly induced, moderate hypothermia aids a patient, along with hypothermia after spinal-fusion surgery.

"This gives us the encouragement to study it more," Green said. "We've seen a dramatic benefit of a trauma (patient) and we've never studied it in a controlled way—and we're going to do it now. Some patients will get the cooling and some won't…and we'll see if it helps."

Added Green: "There is an opportunity for people. Is it raising expectations, or should we just go around and say, 'Spinal injuries (are) forever, people never get better, there's nothing you can do.' Those are your two choices, which would you take?"

Doing the controlled studies won't be easy. After all, it will be difficult to have patients administered hypothermia as quickly as Kevin. How many people are injured in an environment that allows them to be immobilized and injected with iced saline 15 minutes after their injury?

Buoniconti agreed that additional research is needed and that it could be painstakingly slow.

"Sometimes, it's better to utilize the therapy that has been researched than not use it at all—at least in the short-term," he said. "How do you hold something back when you think it's going to be beneficial to somebody?"

To Buoniconti, current research already demonstrates that there are benefits to hypothermia.

"People say to me, 'When will you find a cure for paralysis?'" Buoniconti said. "I say to them, 'Go ask Kevin Everett and he'll tell you we've already found one.'"

Buoniconti, 41, who has spent more than half his life in a wheelchair, is hopeful he will also be able to walk again someday.

"I know the euphoria of making a tackle on fourth and one. I've done that," he said. "I can only imagine the kind of glory I'd get by getting out of a wheelchair.... My goal is to get people out of these chairs."

Gibbons said there were several factors that contributed to Kevin's recovery.

"The care on the field, steroids, and the rapidity in which we got the pressure off the spinal cord," he said. "They were as important—or more important—than the hypothermia because Kevin's critical first movements occurred before we even started effective cooling."

In addition to receiving steroids in the ambulance after he was taken off the football field, Kevin was kept on a steroid drip for 24 hours after his surgery.

Steroids pose a risk of side effects in spinal-cord patients, such as gastrointestinal, lung, and wound infections, Gibbons said. But in this case, the steroids proved beneficial.

Green is not a big proponent of steroids and their effectiveness in treating spinal-cord injuries, but he wondered if perhaps the combination of the steroids and the hypothermia treatment produced the favorable results.

"The only way to find out is to do the research," he said, "and we have a new level of interest and enthusiasm since Kevin's injury. His recovery has been the impetus for it.'"

There has been no human control group to determine hypothermia's effect.

"I've seen others without the saline method who have recovered," said Rafferty Laredo, the occupational therapist at TIRR.

Cappuccino simplified the treatment's effect.

"Think of it like the kid who gets kicked in the shin playing soccer. The quicker you get ice on it, the quicker the swelling goes down," he said.

❖❖❖

You can debate for weeks and not really know if hypothermia played an integral part in Kevin's recovery. What you *can't* debate is that an amazing series of events occurred that seemed to make him destined to recover.

• Buffalo is one of a handful of NFL teams that has a spine specialist on its staff. Hence, Cappuccino was on the sideline, ready to spring into action, when Kevin suffered his injury.

• Kevin played his college ball in Miami, home of the Miami Project, the world's largest comprehensive spinal-cord research center.

"Everything just lined up."

• Buffalo is one of a few teams that has iced saline available.

• Two days before Everett's injury, Cappuccino had gone to Millard Fillmore Gates Hospital to assist one of his son's high school football teammates who had been injured. While there, he noticed the hospital had the capability to do MRIs 24 hours a day—and that is why he instructed the ambulance driver to head to that hospital.

The ability to have an MRI done right away—instead of waiting perhaps two hours for a technician to come into the hospital—was one of the many developments that worked in Kevin's favor.

• Nine days before the injury, the Bills' medical personnel and paramedics went through a spinal-cord drill. Just in case.

• Bills president Ralph Wilson has been a longtime supporter of the Miami Project, which held a hypothermia seminar that Cappuccino attended in 2006. The seminar planted a seed.

"Everything just lined up," Cappuccino said.

Destiny? A player who suffered a catastrophic injury may have been cured by the research done at his university—and that research was funded, in part, by his employer.

Wilson, the Bills' owner and founder, downplayed the role his donations—a reported $2.5 million to the Miami Project—played in Kevin's recovery, calling it "a coincidence." He observed Kevin's dedication when he watched him rehabbing from a torn ligament in his left knee, an injury Kevin suffered during the first day of the Bills' minicamp in 2005, his rookie year.

"I got to know him causally," Wilson said. "I remember seeing him in the training room in his second year here. He was trying to rehab his knee and I saw him jumping around on one leg and doing exercises to try to make a comeback. I said to him, 'Kevin, you're really going after it.'"

Kevin smiled and kept on working...just like he did after his spinal injury.

When he returned to Buffalo late in the 2007 season, Kevin met with Wilson in the owner's suite. "I couldn't believe how wonderful he looked. I was actually amazed at his recovery," Wilson said. "He's so full of spirit and such an inspiration to the whole country."

In an interview with MSG Interactive, Hall of Fame linebacker Nick Buoniconti, the former Miami Dolphins great who is Marc's father, described the circumstances around Everett's treatment as "fortuitous." Nick Buoniconti and Dr. Green cofounded the Miami Project.

Buoniconti noted that Everett attended the University of Miami, "and the doctor who treated him went to the Miami Project seminar and saw the research and had the brains and intuition to use it right away," he said. "The fact that the Miami Project is involved gives me a great feeling that after all these years of hard work and raising money, we're finally doing something that is productive to human beings."

Since his son's injury, Nick Buoniconti has devoted his life to raising money to help find a cure for paralysis. With both Buonicontis and Green leading the way, more than $200 million has been raised for research, and about 200 scientists, doctors, and researchers are working together in Miami to find a cure.

Over the years, progress has been made. The growing of cells to repair damaged spinal cords has returned promising results in tests performed on rats, the Miami Project has reported. The research center's scientists have also been exploring new ways to promote the regrowth of injured nerves and the repair of nerve pathways so communication between the brain and paralyzed regions of the body can be restored.

The science may take years, even decades, before it helps humans.

That's why doctors such as Green are so excited about Kevin's recovery. It gives scientists data that can jump-start their studies and lead to improvements in spinal-cord treatment.

❖ ❖ ❖

The advances made by research scientists also excite those who have been living with spinal-cord injuries, such as Dean Ragone, 50, a Haddonfield, New Jersey, resident who owns a general contracting company that specializes in repairing buildings that have been damaged by disasters such as fires, floods, and hurricanes.

For several terrifying seconds, he thought he was going to drown.

Ragone was paralyzed after a swimming pool accident in 1974. He is confined to a wheelchair, but it hasn't prevented him from moving on with his life. Ragone is married with two children and, in addition to running his business, does volunteer work for the Adam Taliaferro Foundation. In 2007, without any fanfare, his company donated a washer and dryer to a poor Camden family that was going through difficult times; one of the family's members, Shykem Lawrence, had been paralyzed while playing in a high school football game.

Looking back at when he broke his neck in 1974, Ragone said, the medical industry "really didn't know the effects of spinal-cord injuries" and how to treat them.

Ragone was 16 when he attended a party at a friend's house in 1974. He was one of the early arrivers, and he decided to take a swim in the above-ground pool. He stood on a platform, took an extra-springy dive and…

"I was a swimmer most of my life and had done some surfing," Ragone said. "So I knew the water. The problem was, I didn't hit the water. I pushed off too hard when I jumped and I hit the other side of the wall.

"I was instantly paralyzed."

He fell facedown and, as he went toward the pool's bottom, wondered if anyone had seen the accident and would come to his rescue. For several terrifying seconds, he thought he was going to drown.

"I could see my arms in front of me, but I had no feeling. I couldn't feel or move," he said.

Ragone estimated he was in the water 30 or 40 seconds and "started to blow bubbles" because he was having difficulty breathing.

"One of my third cousins pulled me out. No one knew what was wrong," he said. "In those days, they didn't know what to do" when someone suffered a spinal injury. "They sat me up in a chair, which was probably the worst thing you could do."

He wasn't bitter, wasn't complaining. He was just retelling the story in a calm, matter-of-fact tone.

"I couldn't feel anything, but I was conscious the whole time."

An ambulance arrived and, a short time later, Ragone remembers thinking he couldn't breathe because he was strapped in too tightly on the gurney.

He later realized it was the injury, not the straps, that caused his breathing problems.

Ragone was taken to the hospital, and he recalls sleeping on "a Ferris-wheel bed—they strap you to it and the bed turns like a Ferris wheel to prevent bed sores."

Because of complications, Ragone didn't have spinal-fusion surgery until about six weeks after his accident. Kevin Everett's spinal-fusion surgery started less than four *hours* after his injury.

Ragone said his injury—a fracture of the vertebrae at the C5/C6 level—was similar to the one suffered by Adam Taliaferro, the former Penn State football player who has overcome paralysis. Ragone thinks if his injury had occurred today, instead of in 1974, he probably would be walking.

"If you fast-forward it 34 years, they would have been able to (reduce) the swelling and prevented a lot of damage," he said.

Today he would have been immobilized and not placed in a beach chair. "That," he said, "put more pressure on the spinal cord."

Ragone said if hypothermia would been available in 1974, he would have gladly volunteered for the treatment.

Hypothermia "makes so much sense when you realize that all the damage is because of swelling," he said. "Anything you can do to prevent swelling and prevent further injury makes perfect sense."

He doesn't feel sorry for himself. Ragone has been happily married for 18 years and he and his wife, Sharon—"a saint," he calls her—have two beautiful children, Jeff, 15, and Gina, 13. He has a thriving business and, when he can, he helps a friend coach a local high school basketball team in South Jersey.

Ragone never looks back. He credits his close-knit family— Ragone and his two brothers and his parents all live in separate houses on the same street—for helping him through some trying times. He noted that one of his brothers, Daniel, became interested in medicine because of his injury and is now a doctor who specializes in trauma injuries.

"I read something one time and I live by it. It said, 'Don't spend today thinking about yesterday.' That's the only way you can live," he said.

When his daughter recently asked him to help with a homework assignment—finding some inspirational quotes—Ragone had a quick response. "I told her, 'The only obstacles in life are those inside your head,' and it's the truth," he said. "You have to look forward. You can't look back."

It is advice that Kevin Everett plans to follow.

❧ ❧ ❧

When Dr. Cappuccino's name is mentioned, Kevin says simply, "I owe him a lot."

Before they forever became linked, Kevin barely knew Cappuccino. In fact, during the preseason, Kevin didn't even know what Cappuccino did.

"I knew of him, but I didn't actually know who he was," he said.

Kevin was walking through the Bills' training room before a preseason game in 2007 when he asked Chris Fischetti, Buffalo's assistant trainer, a question about the bald-headed man on the other side of the room.

"Who is that guy and what does he do?" Kevin wondered a few weeks before the season opener against the Denver Broncos.

Fischetti told him it was Dr. Cappuccino, a spine specialist who was the team's orthopedic surgeon.

"I don't know why, but I thought to myself, 'I didn't know he was that serious,'" Kevin recalled. "There are several doctors on the staff, and he was the only doctor I really didn't know and didn't know what he did...I've been here three years, and on that day in particular, I had to find out what he did."

It was as if, in a roundabout way, he was preparing to have a connection with the person whom many credit with saving his life.

"I'm not so sure it's a medical miracle, but, for me, it's a victory for a young male athlete," Cappuccino said. "As a physician, I couldn't be happier. Kevin's a great kid—pleasant, unassuming. And you can see he gets his strength from his mom. I spent some time with her and she's quite a lady, and you can't underestimate the importance that she played. She was always there for him."

❖❖❖

Adam Taliaferro, the former Penn State cornerback, said hypothermia was never an option when he was paralyzed while playing at Ohio State in 2000. Taliaferro made a remarkable recovery but still has nerve damage to his hand and walks with a limp.

"It sounds like an amazing protocol and hopefully it'll help others," he said of the treatment.

But he emphasized he was not bitter that the treatment wasn't available for him.

"I had perfect care," he said.

Kevin's injury seemed to be the reason the NFL announced in December that it had awarded a $113,000 grant to the Miami Project to Cure Paralysis, which played a role in the tight end's recovery from paralysis. The Miami Project will use the grant to increase its cutting-edge research into hypothermic therapy, a spokesman announced.

The NFL steadily funded the center from 1986 to 2003; it decided to resume funding at a league meeting in October—the month after Everett's injury.

"As a physician, I couldn't be happier."

Green called the NFL's grant "a step in the right direction. It means that they acknowledge what we've done for Kevin, so we're thrilled to have our foot in the door. And maybe it's an opportunity to work more with them."

Green thinks that Kevin's progress emphasizes the need for further research into treating patients with spinal-cord injuries.

Kevin's recovery "kicks us into gear," Green said. "Hopefully, it'll be a catalyst for all of us to look a little harder inside ourselves and see what we can do about making this available quicker and to more people."

A few months before the NFL awarded the grant to the Miami Project, Marc Buoniconti was miffed by the league's lack of support. He called it "irresponsible," said it was "unfair to the current players," and a "slap in the face to my father and any player who goes on the field and has the potential to have a spinal-cord injury."

"Initially, they were supportive of the Miami Project, but years ago they just pulled the plug on us and started denying our grants," he said. "We're on the verge of clinical trial in humans.... I'm hopeful they will rethink their position."

After Everett's injury, they did.

"The NFL has been focusing on concussions, and I say I'd rather have a concussion than a spinal-cord injury," Buoniconti said.

❖❖❖

James "Junior" Nico, who helped raise Kevin, has a special place in his heart for hypothermia and any of the other methods that played a role in his grandson's recovery.

"I thought we were going to lose him," he said, "but modern medicine helped a lot. Can't say enough about it."

And Patricia, whose pecan pie used to make Kevin lick his lips when he was a youngster, can't say enough about her son.

"I'm so proud of him," she said. "When I see him walking around, when I see him standing tall, when I look at him…I want to bust out crying."

She paused.

"I always felt that he was going to get up and start walking. In my heart, I did. I'm real proud of him, real proud. He's a strong young man, you know. He has a lot of courage and a lot of intensity."

Mamawa Moore, Kevin's future mother-in-law, sent out prayer requests at her church and a school when Kevin was injured.

"Everybody was praying for him," she said. "At my school, where I had taught before, every student, teacher, administrator, and staff (member) were praying for Kevin. But Kevin put our faith into action. He was always willing to try his best. No matter how tired he was, he would do exactly what the doctors and nurses told him to do. He has the will and determination to give 110 percent every single day of his rehab."

Wayetu Moore, a Howard University student who is Kevin's future sister-in-law, said she was "beyond the emotion of pride" when seeing him walk around the house. "I am overwhelmed with joy and inspiration. I am overwhelmed with his story. And I am ecstatic at the opportunity God has granted him to share his testimony to hopefully inspire others. He is so strong, so humble. And I think that it is his humility, his normalcy, that will inspire an entire generation of people who are so used to taking things for granted.

"People can see themselves in him and his story. He's a normal guy who accomplished the Little League dream of the NFL...and then in an instant, it was gone."

The same thing, she said, can happen to anyone. The person may not be a professional athlete, but they can attain a life-long goal in another field and have it taken away in the snap of a finger.

It happened to Kevin, and he was fortunate to have a loving family to help him through the ordeal.

"I thought we were going to lose him, but modern medicine helped a lot. Can't say enough about it."

"The first thing I noticed when visiting Kevin at the hospital in Buffalo was that there was always someone around him," Wayctu said. "He always had family speaking to him, encouraging him and reminding him of how blessed and loved he was."

Wiande and her spiral notebook were never far from Kevin's reach.

"I think the role Wiande played in Kevin's recovery was her consistency," Wayetu said. "She was consistent in caring and loving him, so he came back to her."

He came back to her, inspired millions, and gave hope to spinal-cord patients everywhere—regardless of the medical reason for his recovery.

A REDEFINED FUTURE

CHAPTER 12

"He has experienced something (amazing), and at this point, he has ears that

are listening…and I think his experience is so important

that people need to hear it. People need to hear about the power

of the human spirit, the power of having people close to you,

the power of being physically fit and knowing that

that has a component of happiness."

197

Kevin Everett figured he'd settle into a long NFL career and that he had a while to figure out another professional path.

That was before The Collision, before his playing career ended, before Sundays were no longer special.

Ever since he was 13 years old, football was a big part of Everett's life. Maybe the fact that he wasn't permitted to play during his Pop Warner years—he was too heavy to make the weight class—made Everett appreciate the game even more when he put on the pads.

And, now, that has been taken away from him.

"To be honest, I'm still trying to come to grips with it. I was really progressing to be real good at what I do, and I was very critical of what I do—watching another tight end and (learning) what I could do better and what I could do in certain situations," said Everett, who, in late December, almost four months after his injury, could stay on his feet for about an hour before getting tired.

"I'm just taking things as they come and focusing on my health and getting better. That's the most important thing."

Will he face the inevitable letdown when it's time to prepare for the 2008 season and he's not at the Bills' two-a-day practices in Rochester, New York?

"It's going to be real tough for me to get over," Kevin said. "It's going to take a while, because of the passion I have for the game and the amount of fun I have when I'm playing it."

The passion may keep him in the game as a coach or in another capacity, though Everett's not sure at what level.

"I don't know what ranks I'd be involved with, but I know I do want to be associated with football in some way," he said, adding that if he coached, he would be "high on discipline."

That doesn't surprise Al Celaya, Kevin's high school coach. When Kevin played at Thomas Jefferson High in Port Arthur, Texas, he thrived in a disciplined environment. "He was always respectful and used 'yes sir' when he answered you," Celaya said.

So where does the polite young man go from here? Will he coach? Fulfill a longtime dream and open a restaurant? Become more active in a shower-cleaning company that he and his friend are trying to expand?

"I'm just taking things as they come and focusing on my health and getting better," Kevin said. "That's the most important thing."

When he does think of his future, he sees himself and Wiande with a house full of kids. He sees a job that that gives him a sense of accomplishment. "I really see myself working for myself," he said. "I had the idea of opening a restaurant on my own, and I have a business partner who has been pushing it. I'm just not sure right now."

The business partner is Kevin's barber, Pat Williams, who two years ago devised specially made plastic sheets that cover shower walls and prevent soap-scum buildup. Kevin and Williams are partners in the product, which is advertised on Houston TV stations and is sold primarily online (www.scumguard.com).

Kevin and Williams are hoping to market the product nationally. If successful, that would fill some of Kevin's time. But he has bigger plans. He wants to keep busy, wants to do some motivational speaking, wants to live every day to the fullest.

And at the end of the day, he realizes, there will be times when he deeply misses football—no matter how busy he keeps himself. There will also be days when he wonders how far his recovery will take him.

"I talked to his family about this even before he left the inpatient program," said Teodoro Castillo, Kevin's attending physician at TIRR in Houston. He told them "it's always going to be a potential problem out there. It all depends basically on Kevin's definition (of recovery).... If it comes to the point where he's not noticing any significant improvement, some patients say, 'Oh, gosh. I'm grateful I'm able to do this.' But for some—and I've seen it in a lot of patients—they have a very high expectation and then they feel depressed because they can't do 100 percent. And that remains to be seen with Kevin. Right now, if you ask him, he still wishes to be a lot stronger and back to normal, but he's coping well, I think, despite the situation."

Aside from making remarkable physical strides since his paralyzing tackle, Kevin seems uncannily secure in his thoughts and actions. In a quiet manner, he exudes confidence, and it wouldn't be surprising to see him become a motivational speaker.

"I told him he has a very important story to tell," said Rafferty Laredo, the TIRR occupational therapist. "He has experienced something (amazing), and at this point, he has ears that are listening...and I think his experience is so important that people need to hear it. People need to hear about the power of the human spirit, the power of having people close to you, the power of being physically fit and knowing that that has a component of happiness."

"Anyone who suffers a catastrophic injury finds out things about themselves that they didn't know."

Those who recover from paralyzing injuries seem to have an air of confidence, an air of invincibility. They are at peace, grateful to be able to walk, grateful to be alive, grateful for the small things—a stroll through a park, a visit around a mall—that most of us take for granted.

Barth Green, the neurosurgeon who cofounded the Miami Project, said he has witnessed many spinal-cord patients discover "a spiritual side" after they recover.

"Anyone who suffers a catastrophic injury finds out things about themselves that they didn't know," he said. "They find new strengths and new abilities that they didn't know they had. It brings out the best in people. Look at Marc Buoniconti."

Buoniconti was paralyzed making a tackle in 1985 and is now an ambassador for the Miami Project.

"When I first met him, he was shy and reserved; he was a college student who was used to playing hard in sports and had to grow up in a damn hurry. You grow up (quickly) when you're on a breathing machine for a year," Green said. "And now he's an articulate spokesman who travels around the world and speaks to kings and presidents about curing paralysis."

Inspired by the cards, letters, videos, and emails of support he has received, Kevin has thought of doing some motivational speaking.

"To see how much people care about an individual that they don't even know, it's been unbelievable," he said. "They touched me and made me feel good with their support."

His family hung some of the supportive letters on the wall when Kevin was in the Buffalo hospital. "I'd look at them every day," he said, "and it would motivate me to move—even though I couldn't move."

Yet.

Florida International coach Mario Cristobal, the University of

> We arrived in Austin (for a mini-getaway) around 11:00 PM Sunday, checked into our hotel downtown, and went to find something to eat for dinner. My sense of direction is okay, but Kevin's is a lot better than mine so with the help of the Navigation System and Kevin in the passenger seat, I knew we would be okay. We ate dinner at IHOP and headed back to the Embassy Suites Hotel.
>
> —Wiande's journal entry, December 30, 2007

Miami's tight-ends coach when Kevin played there, has watched replays of the life-altering tackle and said it "didn't look like something that would cause such a dramatic injury. Fortunately, he's back on his feet and he's one guy who will be successful in whatever he does."

Told that Everett is considering lots of options, including coaching, Cristobal smiled broadly. "If so, make sure he gets down here with me," he said. "I'd have him on our staff in a minute. Right now."

If Kevin isn't coaching, Cristobal said, he will ask him to visit with his Florida International players.

"I get excited and fired up just talking about him," Cristobal said. "I want him speaking to our guys. When he's in a room, his presence just takes over."

Virgil Calhoun feels the same way.

"Kevin has a positive attitude and I know he's going to go far in life with his attitude," said Calhoun, Everett's workout buddy at the Houston rehab hospital. "I think he's going to help a lot of people who are going through disabilities. He can relate to it and I know he'll be able to encourage them to do well."

"I hope he can run and play in the park with his kids; that'll be his biggest success."

"So much has happened to Kevin over the last few months and he'll have to reassess his goals," said Jimmy Rieves, Kevin's junior college coach at Kilgore. "Maybe he'll use his experiences to help others, whether it's in public speaking or with the NFL. No matter what he does, he'll be successful because of his attitude and the type of person he is."

Whatever Kevin is doing, he plans to spend a lot of time with what he hopes is a big family. He and Wiande would like to have five children, and they have all the ingredients to be wonderful parents. They are caring, patient, and kind, they have their spirituality to lean on, and they have the confidence, determination, and a sense of indestructibility that develops when you look death and paralysis in the eye...and fail to blink.

"We're going to have a big family. I know that for sure," Wiande said. "And I see us traveling, traveling around the world. I really want to help people and help his foundation."

Kevin will spend time building his foundation and "building relationships," as he likes to say. He will continue to draw strength from recovering from a freakish, life-changing football injury, and he will find work that inspires him—and others—in whatever field

"I'd have him on our staff in a minute. Right now."

he chooses. He was going to start spreading the inspiration right away, starting with an appearance on *The Oprah Winfrey Show.* Other national appearances were in the works.

"I can't see how he'll miss in life," said Tom Modrak, the Bills' director of college scouting and the man who oversaw the selection of Kevin in the 2005 NFL Draft. "He'll be a great family man. I hope he can run and play in the park with his kids; that'll be his biggest success.... What more could you want?"

❖ ❖ ❖

There was some comic relief early in Kevin's recovery, though at the time it didn't seem amusing.

In West Palm Beach, Florida, the sportscaster was introduced as the sports segment of the newscast began:

Now...News12 sports with Pat Murphy.

Murphy, in a highly energized tone, gave viewers a startling update:

"Great news regarding Bills tight end Kevin Everett," he

proclaimed. "He moved his arms and legs and doctors now believe…"

Murphy's voice started to trail off as he realized what he was saying did not reflect the video that his viewers were watching.

"When I talk to Kevin now, I can see it brought him to a place in life, a happy place."

As Murphy talked about Everett's prognosis, viewers watched a man in a wheelchair being pushed by an overweight police officer in a Columbus, Ohio, courtroom. The man began violently kicking at his attorney and quickly fell out of his wheelchair. There was a lot of screaming, a lot of commotion, as three policemen tried to restrain the man, who had been charged with robbing a church.

As he finished his report on Everett's progress, Murphy sheepishly told viewers, "That's the wrong video, by the way. That is not the right video."

Later that night, the video blooper was shown on MSNBC's "Oddball" segment with Keith Olbermann.

"A local news item on injured Buffalo Bills tight end Kevin Everett's miraculous recovery from a spinal injury turned into a sportscaster's worst nightmare…and the viewers'." Olbermann explained to his audience.

Almost as an afterthought, Olbermann told viewers that Everett was able to move his extremities, "and there's hope for significant recovery."

There was no word on the condition of the arrested man who fell out of his wheelchair.

❖ ❖ ❖

As strange as it sounds, Kevin Everett is a happier person today than he was before his injury. That's the opinion of one of his best friends, Robert Royal, a Buffalo Bills tight end who lives in New Orleans.

"I truly believe everything happens for a reason," said Royal, who just finished his sixth NFL season and his second with the Bills. "When I talk to Kevin now, I can see it brought him to a place in life, a happy place. I'm so proud of what he's overcome.

"We love this game and work hard to be the best at it, but life is more important than football. I see him so motivated now, so full of life and energy. The walking and the steps he's taking, they're wonderful, but to listen to him and see how much happier he is with his family and fiancée…that's what excites me. I definitely think he's happier now (than before the injury). In football, things are real stressful; you're trying to figure out where you're going to play and all that. Kevin is competitive and he's going to miss it, but overall, you listen to him and listen to his goal and see how happy he is, that's the part I love about it."

Royal isn't surprised that Kevin is walking again.

"Being the type of person I am, I was always confident about the outcome," he said.

After the September 9 game in which Kevin was injured, Royal recalled, a reporter cornered him in the locker room. "He told me he had inside information that Kevin was going to be paralyzed," Royal said. "I told him I didn't want to be rude, but I didn't want to talk about it because in my mind, he will move and walk again. It just goes to show you how much heart and determination can take you to the next level."

That and a lot of help from two of the women in his life, Wiande and Patricia.

"They've done whatever it takes to get Kevin to this point," Royal said, "and it takes special people to do that. To have them by his side and stick by him is a true blessing. It's amazing that there are people like that to have with you."

Paul Lancaster, the Bills' executive who served as a liaison between the Bills and Everett's loved ones during the crisis, thinks Kevin will be successful in whatever field he pursues.

"You know what? Kevin can do *anything* he wants to do," Lancaster said. "The way he came back and worked—not only the physical aspect but the emotional aspect—is a credit to him. He fought through it and showed that if you put your mind to it, you can accomplish anything in this world."

Kevin will take that resolve into his next job, whether it's in football, public speaking, the restaurant business, or another field.

"Kevin always talked about coaching and working with children," Lancaster said. "I think he can do whatever he puts his mind to."

"He's a smart guy and, more than anything else, he has the drive to be what he wants to be," said Philadelphia Eagles linebacker Takeo Spikes, a former teammate of Kevin's when they were with the Bills. "He'll be a success, with or without football."

"I believe in him," said Trent Edwards, Buffalo's quarterback, "and when you see what he's done and all the progress he's made...how can he not (be a success)? Mentally and physically, he's one of the strongest people I've ever been around, and I think he can be whatever he wants to be."

Even president of the United States?

"I'd vote for him," Edwards said.

Some of the Bills envision Kevin going into business, some see him traveling around the country to share his inspiring story as a motivational speaker, and some see him working with a football team in some capacity.

"Hopefully he'll be doing something he likes and making a lot of money," said a smiling John McCargo, the Bills' 301-pound defensive tackle.

"With the heart and desire he has, how can he *not* be a success?" asked Brian Moorman, the Bills' punter. "And I'm excited to see what the future holds for him."

"I see him being very successful because of the way he carries himself," Bills wide receiver Roscoe Parrish said. "I see him probably working with kids. He's good with people; he's a people person."

The opportunities are endless, Bills cornerback Jabari Greer said.

"People get the idea—and I think we do as players, sometimes—that we can't be successful in anything outside of football," Greer said. "But there's so much out there and so many opportunities, and I know that by the way he's fighting and handling adversity that he'll be successful. He'll be a wonderful husband and father, and he'll have success, maybe more off the field than on it."

> *"You know what? Kevin can do anything he wants to do."*

Kevin's mom agreed.

"He's real smart, and mentally and physically, he's real strong," Patricia Dugas said. "I see him doing a lot of good things in this life. I see him helping others. You just watch him."

Patricia said her son taught her family a valuable lesson: "Just always think positive and keep praying hard," she said. "When you're facing a problem in your life, just never give up and don't let it get you down. Just keep working hard, keep working hard."

❖ ❖ ❖

Injury-plagued Buffalo lost its final three games and finished with a 7–9 record, its third straight losing season. Did Everett's injury cast a negative vibe on the year?

"It didn't have an effect on our record, but it definitely had an effect on our season," said McCargo, the massive defensive lineman. "He was always on your mind and always in your heart.

When it first happened, it had a big effect because you're not focusing on playing but on him getting better."

"I just feel like things would have been different if I could have been there."

"I think the fact that Kevin showed continual improvement was a big positive for us," Bills coach Dick Jauron said. "When he went down—and the aftermath—was painful for everyone. It was painful for Kevin and his family and our team. Kevin is a really good guy and everybody is very close to him. The fact he got better made it an unbelievable blessing.

"He worked awfully hard and the medical staff worked hard… and we got lucky."

Like many of his teammates, Buffalo linebacker Mario Haggan said Everett's injury probably played a role in the Bills' season-opening 15–14 loss to the Broncos. "The Denver game may have had an effect," he said. "We had to battle through that game and we didn't have him here to help our offense. But the team rallied behind him (after the opener) and every play we ran, we did it for him, hoping he was watching."

The Bills' coaches didn't exploit the injury and use it as a rallying cry. The players made it their own rallying point. The Bills overcame a 1–4 start and moved into playoff contention after they trounced the Miami Dolphins, 38–17, and improved their record to 7–6 on December 9.

But the Bills—whose franchise has featured players such as O.J. Simpson, Jim Kelly, Bruce Smith, Thurman Thomas, Joe De-Lamielleure, Billy Shaw, Andre Reed, and Fred Smerlas—had too many injuries to overcome. They limped away with three straight losses, missing the playoffs for the eighth consecutive season.

Though Everett's injury was, by far, the most serious, Buffalo had 17 players on its injured reserve list when it lost its season finale in Philadelphia, 17–9.

"We had a lot of injuries, but every team has them and you have to find a way to overcome them," Jauron said.

"I wish things could have been a whole lot better," Everett said. "I just feel like I could have helped my team. I'm not saying I would have changed a whole lot, but that's just an opinion I have inside. I just feel like things would have been different if I could have been there."

The season wasn't a bust. Several up-and-coming players, like rookie running back Marshawn Lynch, made their mark. And Everett's injury did have a positive: it fostered a strong team unity that can be carried into next season.

"I think it brought us closer, to be honest," said Edwards, the rookie quarterback who was a third-round draft selection out of Stanford. "We had the situation early with Kevin, and at that point, not all the guys knew each other well. We had just gone through camp and the preseason, and when Kevin went down, we kind of came together as a team and rallied around our leaders."

The team's harmony couldn't mask its offensive shortcomings. Buffalo finished with just 20 offensive touchdowns—a team record for a 16-game season. The previous low was 22 touchdowns in 1985, when running back Greg Bell provided most of the offense during a 2–14 season.

The Bills missed Kevin's presence, Greer said.

"Kevin's a guy who's always level-headed and just a smooth guy who has a lot of respect around the locker room," Greer said, "and when it happened and we lost him, the whole team pulled together for him. The coaching staff set up different ways we could communicate with him—we made video messages on Tuesdays and sent the DVDs to him. We were always thinking about him."

"

Today is New Year's Eve and our first New Year's together. I woke up around 8:30 AM and headed to the breakfast lounge with my little sister, Kula, to get breakfast. Kevin was under the weather a little, so we brought our food and his food to the room. Kevin and I always take care of each other. When I'm sick, Kevin goes to the drug store, buys almost every medicine on the shelf to make sure I get better. I do the same for him. So now that he's sick, I went to the store and bought him medicine. (Theraflu Daytime/Nighttime, Tylenol Cold and Flu, Vicks Vapor Rub, honey and lemon cough drops, Alka-Seltzer, etc.). I made sure after he ate breakfast that he took his medicine before we headed out.

Later, we went to dinner at Benihana's Restaurant. We ate and headed downtown to bring in the New Year. Around 11:00 PM we walked along the Congress Bridge toward downtown about one mile. As we walked, we saw a parade going on, kids playing and laughing with one another, and live bands playing music into the New Year. It was about 45 degrees outside and windy, but this was the first time I actually didn't mind the cold air because I had my heart right next to me, by my side. We arrived at a lounge in Austin about 20 minutes before it was New Year's. When we arrived, a woman came and gave my sister, Kevin, and I some horns and confetti to bring in the New Year. The next thing I heard was a man playing on the guitar. Then I heard him count down...10–9–8–7–6–5–4–3–2–1...HAPPY NEW YEAR! We all shouted 'HAPPY NEW YEAR!' and blew our horns. I looked at Kevin and then looked up toward the sky and said, 'Thank you, God' because this indeed was a very happy New Year for the both of us. It was happy not only because it was our first New Year together, but it was happy and blessed because I have my love in my world...in my life still. This past year I almost lost the love of my life, my fiancé, and soon-to-be husband, but God spared his life for a purpose and I'm so thankful as we go into this New Year together for that. Then...we kissed and danced the night away.

—Wiande's journal entry, December 31, 2007 and January 1, 2008

"

"It definitely was (in) the back of everyone's mind the whole season," Moorman said of Everett's injury. "Nothing would ever stop that."

The injury "brought the reality of the game to you real quick," said Royal, who was one of two tight ends—Kevin was the other—in the Bills' starting lineup in the 2007 season opener, "and caused (the players) to get their priorities in order, because on any given play, your career could be over."

> *"Anything is possible. Just don't give up on goals you set for yourself. It's all in God's plan what you were set out to do."*

By early January—nearly four months after the injury—Kevin was able to watch replays of his career-ending tackle and not cringe. Or scream. That wasn't the case during his early days at the Buffalo hospital.

"It wasn't a good time for me back then," Kevin said. "It was fresh and it was just a painful time to look at it again—like I could feel it again. Now that I'm walking again, I'm not bothered by it at all. I'm away from it."

He is now walking and, although his hands are still mostly numb, he has surpassed most of the doctors' projections. In sports parlance, he has *overachieved*.

"Don't let anybody tell you what you can't do," Kevin said. "Anything is possible. Just don't give up on goals you set for yourself. It's all in God's plan what you were set out to do."

As the new year began, Kevin continued his outpatient rehab in Houston, with Wiande still by his side. Because of his progress, the rehab had been reduced from five days a week to three, a development that seemed unthinkable a few days after his surgery, when Kevin developed a bad case of pneumonia and had a paralyzed diaphragm.

"He tried to die a couple times," said Kevin Gibbons, the doctor who managed Kevin's post-operative care at the Buffalo hospital.

Patricia had returned to caring for her three girls and making special meals for Kevin at home.

As for Kevin's sisters, they were back on their usual routine—attending school and doing things with their friends. They no longer worried about Kevin's health, no longer were spending lots of time with him at the hospital.

Herchell, who has aspirations of becoming a pediatrician or a nurse, is finishing 10th grade; Kelli is finishing her freshman high school year and is "the girly-girl of the family—into makeup and getting her hair done," Kevin said; and Davia, who went into a diabetic coma in August, is healthy, singing in the school choir, and completing sixth grade.

All are happy to have their big brother, their confidante, back in their house. Hanging out and watching a movie together in their family room didn't seem like such a big deal in early September. It does now.

"Everything's back to normal around here, and that feels good," Patricia said. "It started out being one of the best years of our lives—we moved into a new house and started a new life—and it ended up being one of our worst years. I was just very happy to see 2007 end."

Wiande decided to extend her leave of absence from her teaching and coaching jobs. She planned to return to Spring High at the start of the new school year in 2008–09. She missed her students and her fellow teachers, but she knew Kevin needed her. And she needed to be with him; she *wanted* to be with him.

A short time after the injury occurred, Wiande met with her parents and told them she wanted to take a leave from school to be with Kevin.

"Follow your heart," they both told her.

So she did. She followed and took part in something that redefined their relationship, redefined their future, redefined their life.

"She was always there for me," Kevin said. "Always."

And she will continue to be. And vice versa.

❖❖❖

Kevin may not be with the team, but he'll "always be a Buffalo Bill," said Royal, the Bills' veteran tight end.

"He wishes he was here with us," Royal said. "He still has that competitive spirit inside him and it's still burning. Unfortunately, he can't be here, but he's going to be...a Buffalo Bill forever."

And, in a way, he'll always be the 12th man in the Bills' huddle. A fan described the inspiration Kevin has provided in a heartfelt letter to *Sports Illustrated*, writing that Kevin "truly represents the city of Buffalo when he states, 'If you get knocked down, you've got to get back up.' With Super Bowl losses, factories closing down, and companies moving away, Buffalo has been getting knocked down for years but keeps getting back up."

The Bills are obligated to pay Everett for a portion of 2008, which was the final season of his four-year contract. His 2008 contract was for $560,000 and, by rule, Kevin is entitled to half of his salary—up to $275,000—in the event of an injury, according to Kevin's agent. Troy Vincent, president of the National Football League Players' Association and a former teammate of Kevin's in Buffalo, said Everett qualifies as a vested veteran by earning his third full NFL season when the Bills placed him on the injured reserve list. That means Everett is eligible for the union's lifetime compensation package for permanent or partial disability, pending a committee's findings.

Kevin isn't concerned with the finances. His focus is on continuing his recovery...and staying connected to the Bills.

"I'll always be around the organization," he said.

Perhaps the Bills will find another job in the organization for Kevin. That remains to be seen.

Many years ago, the Bills received their nickname from a contest in which a fan wrote that, while the legendary Indian scout William "Wild Bill" Cody helped trailblaze the American Frontier, the football team—owned by the president of Frontier Oil—was opening a new frontier in Buffalo sports.

"I think God has another chapter for Kevin in his life and needs him to pursue something else; he already has done what he needs to do in football."

With that in mind, it seems fitting that Kevin Everett made his remarkable recovery while a member of the Buffalo Bills, starting a new frontier for the treatment of spinal-cord injuries and making his name synonymous with miracles of the medical kind.

Wiande preferred to think of it as another sort of miracle.

"I truly believe it was God who helped the doctors. They say it's a miracle. Yes, it is a miracle, but it is God's miracle, and everything happens for a purpose and a reason," she said. "I want to give the glory to God. I think God has another chapter for Kevin in his life and needs him to pursue something else; he already has done what he needs to do in football."

What he did teaches us about heart, teaches us about resiliency, teaches us about what can be accomplished with a loving family by your side.

And, perhaps most important of all, it teaches us about the power of the indefatigable human spirit.

PHOTO CREDITS

Color section 1
Page 1   Photos courtesy of Kevin Everett
Page 2   Top: Photo courtesy of Kevin Everett; Bottom: Photo by Vince Gallico, courtesy of Kevin Everett
Page 3   Top and bottom: Photos courtesy of Kevin Everett; Middle: Photo by Vince Gallico, courtesy of Kevin Everett
Page 4   Photos courtesy of Getty Images
Page 5   Photos courtesy of Getty Images
Page 6   Top: Photo courtesy of Getty Images; Bottom: Photo courtesy of AP/Wide World
Page 7   Photo courtesy of Getty Images
Page 8   Top: Photo courtesy of Getty Images; Bottom: Photo courtesy of AP/Wide World Photos

Color section 2
Page 1   All photos courtesy of AP/Wide World Photos
Page 2   Top and middle: Photos courtesy of AP/Wide World Photos; Bottom: Photo courtesy of Getty Images
Page 3   Top: Photo courtesy AP/Wide World Photos; Bottom: Photo courtesy of Kevin Everett
Page 4   Photos courtesy of Kevin Everett
Page 5   Photos courtesy of Sam Carchidi
Page 6   Photos courtesy of Sam Carchidi
Page 7   Top left and right: Photos courtesy of Getty Images; Bottom: Photo courtesy of AP/Wide World Photos
Page 8   Photos courtesy of Tim Fulton Photography

In main text
Page 1   Photo courtesy of AP/Wide World Photos
Page 15   Photo courtesy of Kevin Everett
Page 29   Photo courtesy of AP/Wide World Photos
Page 45   Photo by Vince Gallico, courtesy of Kevin Everett
Page 61   Photo courtesy of AP/Wide World Photos
Page 83   Photo courtesy of Kevin Everett
Page 101 Photo courtesy of Kevin Everett
Page 117 Photo courtesy of Kevin Everett
Page 137 Photo courtesy of AP/Wide World Photos
Page 153 Photo courtesy of Kevin Everett
Page 175 Photo courtesy of AP/Wide World Photos
Page 197 Photo courtesy of Tim Fulton Photography

ABOUT THE AUTHOR

Sam Carchidi has been a sportswriter and columnist at *The Philadelphia Inquirer* since 1984. He has written for several national publications, and he was one of *The Philadelphia Inquirer* reporters who contributed to the book *Worst to First: The Story of the 1993 Phillies*.

In 2001, he and Scott Brown coauthored the nationally acclaimed *Miracle in the Making: The Adam Taliaferro Story*. Carchidi wrote *Bill Campbell: The Voice of Philadelphia Sports* in 2006.

Carchidi, a Rowan University (formerly Glassboro State College) graduate, lives in Wenonah, New Jersey, with his wife, JoAnn; their children, Sara and Sammy; and his mother-in-law, Maryann.